BORN CURIOUS

20 Girls Who Grew Up to Be
AWESOME SCIENTISTS

MARTHA FREEMAN • illustrated by KATY WU

A PAULA WISEMAN BOOK

Simon & Schuster Books for Young Readers • New York London Toronto Sydney New Delhi

For Penelope, who was born curious
—M. F.

For my mentee, Jaileen, and the Nieves family
—K. W.

SIMON & SCHUSTER BOOKS FOR YOUNG READERS

An imprint of Simon & Schuster Children's Publishing Division

1230 Avenue of the Americas, New York, New York 10020

Text copyright © 2020 by Martha Freeman

Illustrations copyright © 2020 by Katy Wu

For information about special discounts for bulk purchases, please contact Simon & Schuster

Special Sales at 1-866-506-1949 or business@simonandschuster.com.

The Simon & Schuster Speakers Bureau can bring authors to your live event. For more information or to book an event,

contact the Simon & Schuster Speakers Bureau at 1-866-248-3049 or visit our website at www.simonspeakers.com.

Book design by Alicia Mikles

The text for this book was set in Bernhard Gothic.

The illustrations for this book were created digitally in Adobe Photoshop.

Manufactured in Hong Kong

1119 SCP

First Edition

2 4 6 8 10 9 7 5 3 1

Library of Congress Cataloging-in-Publication Data

Names: Freeman, Martha, 1956– author. | Wu, Katy, illustrator.

Title: Born curious : 20 girls who grew up to be awesome scientists / by Martha Freeman ; illustrated by Katy Wu.

Other titles: Girls who grew up to be awesome scientists

Description: First edition. | New York : Simon & Schuster Books for Young Readers, [2020] | "A Paula Wiseman Book." |

Audience: Ages 7–12. | Audience: Grades 4 to 6. | Includes bibliographical references and index.

Identifiers: LCCN 2019008763 | ISBN 9781534421530 (hardcover : alk. paper) | ISBN 9781534421547 (eBook)

Subjects: LCSH: Women scientists—Biography—Juvenile literature.

Classification: LCC Q141 .F74 2020 | DDC 509.2/52—dc23

LC record available at https://lccn.loc.gov/2019008763

CONTENTS

INTRODUCTION

IN THESE PAGES YOU'LL read about twenty scientists who changed the way we understand the universe.

Boring, right?

Wrong!

Whether they studied galaxies far away or fruit fly cells, the structure of a virus or the structure of the stratosphere, the behavior of a billiard ball or the behavior of a Komodo dragon—all of these women woke up eager to make discoveries every day.

And for us, that's a very good thing. Without these women, people would know a lot less, and the world would be a sicker, dirtier, more dangerous place.

From ancient times until today, women have pursued science and math, even if their contributions weren't always recognized. We chose the women in this book because they do different kinds of science, and because each of their stories is different. Some grew up rich and others poor. Some grew up in peaceful circumstances, and others in times or places torn by conflict. Some were the smartest kids in the class, while others struggled to find something they were good at.

As women in professions dominated by men, some felt discrimination, while others said they were usually able to shrug it off.

One thing they had in common: They were born curious.

Are you curious too? Read on.

Then get up, get out, and do some science of your own!

ELLEN SWALLOW RICHARDS

GEOCHEMIST

1842-1911

MARCH IS THE QUIETEST month on the farm near Dunstable, Massachusetts, so every year the family takes a break and visits relatives in Vermont, Maine, and New Hampshire. The distances are short, but this is the 1840s, and the only way to travel is by wagon. Every trip becomes an adventure.

Bumping along in the back, tucked in blankets, the little girl with the serious gray eyes listens to her parents argue. Mama—always a worrier—says the still-snowy road is too dangerous, and they should turn back. But Papa, driving the team of horses, says that's nonsense. The roads are well-traveled and, "Where any one else has been, there I can go."

All her life, the girl will remember this motto of her papa's and think that while it's true enough, it doesn't really suit her. What she wishes for herself is an adventurous spirit, one tough enough to do things no one else has ever done.

As a child, though, Ellen Henrietta Swallow—known as Nellie—was kept plenty busy with routine chores at home. Her mother got sick a lot. Her father had his hands full with the farm, which never brought in much money. It was up to Nellie to cook, wash, iron, clean, and even hang wallpaper.

Nellie liked some of the work and took pride in doing it well. By the time she was ten, her embroidery and her baking had won prizes at the county fair.

Nellie's pursuits were not confined to the house. She also drove the cows to pasture, pitched hay and—best of all—kept a garden. All her life Nellie loved flowers and plants. In a letter to her cousin and best friend, Annie, she bragged about her amaryllis and geraniums.

Nellie was good at schoolwork, especially Latin, and when she graduated from the Westford Academy—the equivalent of today's high school—she wanted more education.

Unfortunately, her family was having the usual money troubles, and there was none to spare for her to go to college.

So Nellie decided to earn the money herself.

By this time her father had opened a general store. She worked the counter, kept the accounts, and went to Boston to buy supplies. She also gave Latin lessons. Most important, she saved like crazy, living for a while on a diet of only bread and milk.

Two years passed, and still Nellie did not have enough money for college. In 1866—when she was twenty-four—the hard work, the scrimping, and the frustration combined to make her sick. Till then Nellie had always been a bundle of energy, but suddenly she couldn't so much as get up off the couch.

Today we would probably call the problem depression. She called it "purgatory, the time when my own heart turned against me."

How she overcame her sickness is not clear, but later she would write, "When you feel an indication of a certain morbid feeling, resolutely set your mind in another direction, and don't give up easily. Let the mind know there is a willpower to control it. This is possible."

By the summer of 1868, she had a plan, which she announced to a friend like this: ". . . I have been to school a good deal, read quite a little, and so secured quite a little knowledge. Now I am going to Vassar College to get it straightened out and assimilated."

Vassar College in New York State was only seven years old and exclusively for women. (Today men attend Vassar too.) Nellie was twenty-five when she enrolled, and from the moment she got there she loved it. Among her professors was the astronomer Maria (pronounced Mar-EYE-ah) Mitchell, whose life story would inspire astrophysicist Vera Cooper Rubin (see page 31) six decades later.

Maria encouraged Nellie to become an astronomer, but Nellie chose to focus on chemistry. She believed being useful was part of her Christian duty. She thought knowing chemistry would make her useful, but she had no idea how.

Nellie researched the chemical composition of iron ore at Vassar, then went to the Massachusetts Institute of Technology (MIT). She was the first woman to earn a degree in chemistry in the United States, and the first woman to study at a technical institute.

ELLEN SWALLOW RICHARDS

In 1875 Nellie married an MIT professor of mining engineering, Robert Richards. The two spent their honeymoon in Nova Scotia with a few friends—Robert's entire class of future engineers. Eventually, the couple would travel all over the world studying rocks, mining, and mineral processing. In 1879, Nellie became the first woman to join the American Institute of Mining and Metallurgical Engineers.

Nellie had worried about money all her life. While doing her graduate studies at MIT, she made ends meet by running the boarding house where she lived. Now she was helped out by her husband's salary and could put her scientific training to work. At last she could be useful the way she had always intended.

Remembering her own frustrations seeking more education, she founded MIT's women's laboratory, a place for science teachers (almost all women) to learn more about the subjects they taught. Soon after that, she developed an advanced chemistry program at the Girls High School in Boston. Later, she would become an instructor of sanitary chemistry at MIT, the first woman to serve on the MIT faculty.

In 1876, she and Robert renovated a house to show off her ideas about environmental and domestic science. Among other things, they installed special windows to improve ventilation, removed lead pipes to clean the drinking water, and built a drip irrigation system for Nellie's beloved houseplants.

Nellie's dedication to bringing science home led her to test foods to determine how nutritious they were, and to calculate exactly how much gas was required to cook different meals. The result of that and similar research was the field now known as home economics, or family and consumer science. Nellie founded the American Home Economics Association and wrote ten books on nutrition, housing, sanitation, and health.

She also helped establish the New England Kitchen, which came up with inexpensive ways to prepare healthy food. From that project came the first school lunch program in the United States.

In 1887, the Massachusetts state department of health asked Nellie to improve drinking water for the people in and around Boston. As usual, she was energetic, working fourteen-hour days, seven days a week, to test some 40,000 water samples and using the results to make a map of water pollution in Massachusetts. Based on her research, the first water quality standards were established in the United States.

Later, Nellie would start a business that analyzed air, food, fabric, mineral oils, and even wallpaper to make sure they were safe.

As a student at MIT, Nellie had done the work for a doctorate in chemistry, but the university refused to give her the degree. It would have been the first graduate degree in chemistry from the school, and some professors thought it would look bad if it went to a woman.

Almost one hundred years later, MIT established a special professorship for a distinguished woman scientist. From 2012 to 2016, climate scientist Susan Solomon (see page 83) was the Ellen Swallow Richards professor at MIT.

ELLEN SWALLOW RICHARDS

Achievement: Geochemist who founded the fields of sanitation engineering and home economics and helped establish the first standards for clean drinking water.

Quote: "You cannot make women contented with cleaning and cooking, and you need not try."

Fascinating fact: In college, Nellie Richards and her friends tried to cure themselves of the habit of using "bad" language, including expressions like "My goodness!" Any time a girl got caught, she had to pay a few cents as penalty. Nellie never had to pay.

JOAN BEAUCHAMP PROCTER

ZOOLOGIST

1897–1931

*E*VEN WHEN SHE'S TINY, the little girl does not care about dolls. Instead she likes animals. Dogs and cats are good. Even better are snakes, toads, lizards, and turtles.

In 1907 when she is ten, her parents let her bring home to London a green Dalmatian wall lizard from a family vacation. She watches the lizard's behavior, and reads everything she can about lizards, too. She is good at art and good with her hands, so she draws a picture of a dream house for her pet. Then she builds it.

Before she gets to work, she thinks hard. What does her lizard like? How much does it like to move around? What and how does it eat?

When she grows up, Joan Beauchamp Procter will do the same thing again but on a much bigger scale. She will design and then help build the reptile house at the London Zoo, the first of its kind anywhere. Almost a century later, it is still in use.

Joan's Dalmatian lizard went with her everywhere, even to the table for tea. Her parents and older sister, Chrystabel, were not necessarily big lizard fans, but they put up with her. Joan had been born with health problems, and she was sick and in pain a lot. *Give her a break,* her family must have thought. *Lizards make Joan happy. Let her have her lizards.*

Not everyone was so tolerant. As a teenager, Joan had a pet crocodile. One day she brought it with her to math class, and something went wrong. Just what is not recorded, but you can bet it involved a set of sharp teeth. Joan was one of the best students at her prestigious private school. Even so, the math teacher was not amused.

That summer the family again went on vacation. With a pale purple ribbon tied around its middle, the crocodile went for walks with Joan. As it grew, she took her questions about its care and feeding straight to the top—the curator of the reptile

collection at one of the biggest and best museums in the world, the British Museum.

The man in charge of the reptile collection, Sir Edward George Boulenger, was so impressed with Joan that he offered her a chance to work with him. Joan's poor health had kept her from going to college, so she agreed, becoming what we'd now probably call an unpaid intern.

For three years at the museum, she did research on herpetology, the study of reptiles. She wrote letters about her research to experts all over the world, earning a reputation as a good scientist. Sometimes she presented what she had learned to other scientists in London, all of them men and all of them older than Joan.

In one of her presentations, she solved a mystery: How did a particular African tortoise manage to live in the crevices of boulders?

Joan's answer: Unlike any other tortoise, it has a flexible shell, which is why it's commonly called a pancake tortoise.

Besides research, the museum allowed Joan to use her artistic talents. She made models of reptiles for public display and painted watercolor pictures that were sold as postcards.

Joan rose fast. In 1924, she took over for Boulenger as curator of reptiles at the London Zoo when he left to head up the London Aquarium. Joan was twenty-five years old, with dark hair and piercing eyes. She was also petite. Some of the snakes and lizards at the zoo were huge. The newspapers loved the story of the first woman zoo curator, and she became a media sensation.

She ignored the attention. She was too busy. Not only did she manage day-to-day care, she also treated the animals' bites and sores. She identified new reptile diseases and found treatments. She operated on the eyes of rattlesnakes and cobras.

Remember how she was good with her hands? There wasn't as much ready-made veterinary equipment then as there is now. Sometimes Joan herself made the instruments required for surgery.

In 1928, two Komodo dragons arrived at the London Zoo from Indonesia. Komodos are a species of lizard that weigh about 150 pounds and grow to more than eight feet long. When they bite, they secrete venom into their prey. The new ones were pretty beat up after being caught and shipped. One of them, a female named Sumbawa, had a mouth infection, which Joan treated herself. She also spoon-fed the lizard eggs and pieces of chicken. Once Sumbawa bit the bowl off the spoon. Oops!

In an essay, Joan wrote that some people thought Komodo dragons were ferocious, but this was nonsense. Instead, the animals had a curious dignity, large, bright, gentle eyes, and the temperament of a big dog. A few weeks after Sumbawa's arrival, Joan hosted a children's tea party with Sumbawa as the star attraction.

Times have changed, and zoologists today would frown on a professional who treated a wild animal like a pet. But Joan was ahead of her time in her sincere regard and respect for the reptiles in her care. Rather than thinking first of their value to humans, she thought first of their health and well-being.

When it was time to design a new enclosure for the reptiles at the zoo, Joan planned every detail, including new kinds of heating, lighting, and window glass to keep the reptiles healthy. Once the design was done, she supervised the construction, making sure the workers got every detail right.

By 1928, Joan's health was getting worse. She tried to quit her job, but her boss wouldn't let her. She was too valuable. So she got around the zoo in a motorized wheelchair, often accompanied by a Komodo dragon on a leash. Joan had come from a prominent, prosperous family. She didn't earn much money, but she lived in a big house near the zoo with a chimpanzee named Johnnie and several reptile pets. There she died in her sleep in 1931 at the age of thirty-four.

Afterward, two species of reptile were named for her: the Uluguru forest snake, *Buhoma procterae*; and the Speke's hinge-back tortoise, *Testudo procterae*. When her colleagues at the London Zoo commissioned a marble bust of her, they placed it near the entrance to the reptile house. There, Joan Beauchamp Procter still greets visitors today.

JOAN BEAUCHAMP PROCTER

Achievement: Zoologist who advanced understanding of reptiles and amphibians, served as curator at the London Zoo, pioneered humane design for zoo habitats, and developed innovative veterinary surgical techniques.

Quote: "It is quite true that (Komodo dragons) are very nervous and quite true that they could no doubt kill one if they wished or give a terrible bite to the hand when taking food greedily, but there is no vice in them."

Fascinating fact: Joan designed not only the reptile house at the London Zoo but also an enclosure for baboons known as Monkey Hill. It was very popular with visitors, but the baboons fought fiercely in the small space, and many died. Eventually it had to be torn down.

FRANCES OLDHAM KELSEY
PHARMACOLOGIST AND PHYSICIAN
1914-2015

THERE ARE NO SCHOOLS in the small town of Cobble Hill on Vancouver Island in Canada, so Mom—Katherine Oldham—takes it upon herself to teach her five-year-old son to read and write.

His sister is two years younger—only three—but what the heck. She might as well pay attention. Soon she gets the hang of reading and writing too.

The girl's name is Frances, but she goes by Frankie. Eventually, she will earn degrees in biology, pharmacology, and medicine, and live a very long life—101 years. Throughout, she will credit inspiring teachers, starting with her mother, for her success.

In the early twentieth century, Vancouver Island was wide open and beautiful. There were no cars yet. Everyone got around by horse and buggy. Frankie herself enjoyed free roam of the place, collecting bugs and the eggs of wild birds.

Frankie was the only girl enrolled at her first real school, which was run by a father and son from Ireland. There she learned a lot of Latin and some algebra and geometry. She also took painting and piano lessons from two talented women who had had professional careers. Her dancing teacher would go on to work in New York City with one of the most famous dancers of the twentieth century, Martha Graham.

Not all Frankie's education was formal. Her best friend, Jerry, taught her to hunt and fish and—when cars finally arrived—to drive a truck, too.

She never told her parents that last part.

Frankie had decided early on she wanted to be a scientist, but the only science class offered at her high school in the nearby city of Victoria was chemistry and, as she wrote later, "Chemistry lost me with the law of mass action."

She was "feeling a bit in the dark and stuck," when a biology professor who was also a family friend took her for a nature walk on the beach. He knew all the animals and plants, including their scientific classifications. He also had suggestions about how she might catch up in school.

Inspired, Frankie took classes at Victoria College for two years, then went to study at McGill University in Montreal.

At McGill, Frankie studied biology and pharmacology—the effect of chemicals on the body. Some of her projects sound kind of crazy. For example, to earn her master's degree, she studied the effect of chemicals secreted by the pituitary gland.

"For a year I sat surrounded by frogs in little cages set in water," she recalled later. "I would lift them up, dry them, weigh them, inject them, put them back in water, and then weigh them at fifteen- to twenty-minute intervals for four hours."

Later, still learning about the pituitary gland, she studied whales, codfish, and armadillos.

In 1936, Frankie left Canada and moved to Chicago to study for her PhD in pharmacology. There, her advisor, Eugene Geiling, asked her to help him with a project. A new liquid medicine that contained an antibiotic called sulfanilamide was being prescribed to treat infections. Because it tasted sweet, it was often given to children with sore throats.

The medicine was popular, but some doctors thought it might be harmful. Days after taking it, many patients got sick; a few had even died. What was going on? To find out, Eugene set up an animal study.

"My job was to watch the rats," Frankie recalled decades later. "I can see them still." What she saw was the poor things getting sick and eventually dying. It wasn't long before the problem became obvious. The chemical used to make sulfanilamide dissolve in liquid was poison.

The company stopped selling the medicine, but many patients had already suffered permanent damage to their kidneys, and about one hundred had died. When the news got out, people demanded that the government do something. In 1938, Congress passed a law requiring any company with a new medicine to show evidence that it was safe before selling it.

Frankie married a colleague, Fremont Ellis Kelsey, in 1943. They had two daughters, and Frankie went back to school for another degree, this one in medicine. The family spent six years in South Dakota, then moved to Washington, D.C., where Frankie took a job as a medical officer with the Food and Drug Administration (FDA).

She is best known for what happened next.

The FDA is the government agency in charge of making sure medicines are safe. Frankie had been there only a month when her boss asked her to look at an application for a license to sell a drug called thalidomide. It was intended to cure nausea and help people—especially pregnant women—sleep.

The drug was already being sold in Europe, so the drug maker figured the FDA would approve its application, no problem.

But Frankie thought the application was incomplete. Instead of including evidence based on scientific studies, it included reviews from doctors saying how great the drug was. Frankie didn't approve the license. She asked for more information.

Executives at the drug company were mad. They had tons of thalidomide in warehouses, ready to sell. They expected to make a lot of money. They visited her office to try to change her mind. They wrote letters. They phoned her boss. They called Frankie "nitpicking" and "unreasonable."

Frankie was tall, but she was not an intimidating person. She spoke quietly and couldn't be bothered with makeup. She was forty-seven years old, and her hair was going gray. People who didn't know her well thought she was shy.

But she wasn't, not really.

She knew bad science when she saw it. And she wouldn't back down.

About three months after the drug maker had submitted its application, Frankie saw a report by a British physician whose patients had taken thalidomide. In some cases, he wrote, it made the nerves in their hands and feet go numb.

Frankie became even more concerned. Working on a malaria treatment fifteen years before, she had seen firsthand how a chemical in a female rabbit's bloodstream could affect its unborn kit. If thalidomide affected the nerves in a woman's hands and feet, what might it do to an unborn child?

Frankie's requests for more information were still holding up the drug's license in late 1961 when news began arriving from hospitals in Europe. Babies were being born with awful birth defects. What did the babies have in common? Their mothers had taken thalidomide.

In the end, more than 10,000 children in Europe and elsewhere were born with deformities caused by thalidomide. Along with FDA colleagues Oyam Jiro and Lee Geismar, Frankie prevented a similar tragedy in the United States.

Newspapers called her a hero, and President John F. Kennedy presented her with an award for public service. In his speech, the president cited Frankie's "high ability and steadfast confidence in her professional decision."

Just as they had in 1938, lawmakers responded by passing new, stricter laws regulating the sale of drugs.

Frankie wasn't done yet. She worked at the FDA for the next forty-three years, rewriting and improving safety rules, many of which were eventually adopted in other countries. She retired in 2005 at age ninety. By then she had lived in the United States for almost seventy years. But the most prominent piece of art in her home was a photo of her childhood home in Cobble Hill.

FRANCES OLDHAM KELSEY

Achievement: Pharmacologist, physician, and public official who saved lives and prevented birth defects by blocking the sale of dangerous drugs.

Quote: "Just stick to your guns."

Fascinating fact: In school, Frankie did research on the pituitary glands of armadillos. Armadillos cannot be bred in a lab, so she drove from Chicago to a Texas ranch, hunted and captured several, then brought them back to her lab to study.

GERTRUDE BELLE ELION
BIOCHEMIST AND PHARMACOLOGIST
1918-1999

O N A SHADY PARK bench, a little girl listens to her grandfather reading a story. Her grandfather's English is good, but his accent is strong. He moved to New York City from Eastern Europe only recently. Even so, you can see from the way they sit together that they are the best of friends.

Gertrude Elion was seven years old when her grandfather, a retired watchmaker, immigrated from Eastern Europe to live with her family. It was 1924, a big year in the little girl's life. Besides her grandfather's arrival, her brother, Herbert, was born, and the family moved from Manhattan to the Bronx.

Gertrude, known as Trudy, was not entirely sure about Herbert. But she liked the Bronx, where there were lots of parks, including the Bronx Zoo. And she loved her grandfather.

Trudy grew up a busy kid with a lot of interests. Her mother, a homemaker, encouraged her to have a career so that she wouldn't have to rely on a husband for money. Trudy was so patient helping her brother with his homework that everyone figured her career would be as a teacher. She was also her father's favorite date to the Metropolitan Opera and a particular fan of music written by the composer Wolfgang Amadeus Mozart.

Trudy read everything. Mystery stories were favorites, and so was a book called *The Microbe Hunters*, published when she was eight years old. This story of the scientists who discovered microbes (tiny organisms, many of them bacteria) was written for adults, but it was so exciting that it inspired Trudy and many other young readers.

Trudy's dad had worked nights in a drugstore so he could go to dental school during the day. Like him, Trudy was a hard worker. She skipped two grades in elementary

school and graduated from high school with honors when she was only fifteen. Her good grades earned her a place at New York City's Hunter College.

Even as a young person, Trudy had confidence and thought she could do something important. But what? The answer came shortly before she started college. Her beloved grandfather got sick and went to the hospital. Trudy visited and saw he was in terrible pain. When he died, she was heartbroken, but she was also set on her path. Her grandfather died of cancer. She determined to be a scientist and fight it.

The next question was what kind of science to study? At first she thought biology, but then she found out biology majors had to dissect animals.

No thank you.

When Trudy graduated with a degree in chemistry, she applied for jobs and got a surprise. Even though she had graduated with honors, she couldn't find one. One person told her that a woman in a lab would distract the men. Much later, she recalled her disappointment: "The world was not waiting for me."

So she went back to school to learn secretarial skills and eventually volunteered to work in a chemistry lab. While finishing up the research for her master's degree at night, she worked as a doctor's receptionist and later taught high school science during the day.

She also fell in love. Leonard Canter was a student, too. He and Trudy became engaged, but heartbreak awaited. Leonard developed an infection. If this had happened only a few years later, penicillin probably would have cured it. But penicillin was not yet available. Leonard died, and Trudy never again had a serious boyfriend. Anytime a young man was interested, she told him she was too busy.

Like geologist Marie Tharp (see page 27), Trudy credited World War II with giving her a break. There was work to be done, some of it in labs. With many men at war, companies had to hire women to do it. Trudy's first full-time job in chemistry was analyzing foods like vanilla beans, pickles, jam, and mayonnaise to make sure they were safe to sell. It was interesting for a while, but it became repetitive. Soon she was looking for something new.

It took time, but she found it at British drug company Burroughs Wellcome, which had a research lab in Tuckahoe, New York. There, a scientist named George Hitchings had a bold idea: Learn more about how cells work, and use that knowledge to stop the ones that cause disease. At last Trudy had the chance to do the work she wanted to do—work that would help fight disease. Her first assignment was to study purines, two kinds of molecules that help transmit genetic information from one cell to the next generation.

When she started, Trudy didn't even know quite what a purine was. So she went to the library. Soon she saw herself as a kind of detective, solving mysteries like the ones she had read as a child. The work required not only chemistry but physiology, biology, and physics. It was exciting and fun—not work at all. In 1949, five years after she took the job, Trudy synthesized a purine that stopped the spread of certain cancer cells in mice.

Would it work in people? In nearby New York City, a doctor treating desperately sick cancer patients rushed to use it. Sadly, the treatment did nothing for some of them, but others got better—at least for a time. Trudy's purine was an early version of 6-mercaptopurine, a kind of chemotherapy still saving lives in the twenty-first century.

Trudy stayed with the same company until 1983, developing drugs to treat cancer, herpes, malaria, and gout. She also developed the first drugs that attacked viruses, as well as treatments to prevent the body's immune system from attacking transplanted organs. All in all, she invented or helped to invent forty-five medical treatments, and wrote more than 200 papers based on her research.

In 1988, she and George shared the Nobel Prize for physiology or medicine with a British scientist, Sir James Black. On stage at the ceremony in Sweden, Trudy's brilliant blue gown stood out among the other award winners—all men in tuxedoes. She stood out for another reason, too. When the orchestra struck up music from an opera by Mozart, everyone else sat stiff and proper, but Trudy smiled and tapped her foot.

GERTRUDE BELLE ELION

Achievement: Biochemist and pharmacologist who identified differences in the way organisms, among them cancer cells and viruses, grow and reproduce, invented medical treatments for cancer, gout, herpes, and many other diseases.

Quote: "Don't let others discourage you or tell you that you can't do it. In my day, I was told women didn't go into chemistry. I saw no reason why we couldn't."

Fascinating fact: Trudy's brother, Herbert, grew up to be a scientist and a businessman. In spite of all Trudy accomplished, her family always considered him the smart one. That changed when she won the Nobel Prize.

ROSALIND FRANKLIN
MOLECULAR BIOLOGIST
1920-1958

HUNCHED IN A CHAIR by a window overlooking the English Channel, a petite dark-haired girl makes tiny, perfect stitches in delicate fabric. Miserably lonely, she is comforting herself the best way she knows how. She is making something.

The girl is nine years old and small for her age. Her parents have sent her to the boarding school on the coast because they think the sea air will be good for her health. If she were home in London, she might be making either a tower from a Meccano building set, or a cupboard from wood, nails, and sandpaper. Stuck at school, she is making a dress for her new baby sister. When she finishes that, she will knit a scarf for her nanny.

From earliest childhood, Rosalind Franklin, known as Rosy, liked to make things and also to know how things were made—what secret structures were hidden inside. Rosy's mother, Bertha, worried about her. Rosy didn't like dolls or playing pretend. Her passion was for real stuff, for facts. As an adult, she would direct that passion toward uncovering the secret structures of coal, living cells, and viruses.

Rosy was born in Great Britain in 1920, during the reign of King George V. Her family was well-off, and when Rosy was three, she was chosen to present a bouquet of flowers to the Duchess of York—later Queen Elizabeth II. The presentation took place at a benefit for a charity school supported by Rosy's parents, who believed in helping others. When the Nazis began persecuting Jews in Germany, her family welcomed Jewish refugees.

Rosy was smart and knew it. When she was six, a visiting aunt described her as "alarmingly clever," noting that she solved arithmetic problems for fun. Her frequent letters to her grandmother included updates on her grades and awards. Once she whined that she would have gotten a better grade except the teacher had added wrong and refused to admit it.

Rosy also had a mischievous streak. At the age of two, she teased her older brother by threatening to put his canary in a sandwich, and her nanny by calling her the worst word she could think of, "dustbin."

Growing up, Rosy tackled challenges of all sorts. She memorized star maps, then searched the night sky to find the constellations. She also loved sports: hockey, squash, tennis, rowing, and cycling. On vacation, she climbed mountains.

Before she was twelve, she had read the Bible cover to cover, searching for proof that God existed. When she was done, she wondered why He couldn't just as well have been a She.

Was Rosy just a teeny bit intense? Her parents thought so. Hoping to calm her down, they gave her a cat, Wilhelmina, who rested on the arm of her chair while she did homework.

Most subjects interested her. In letters about school, she described "a lovely discussion of gravity and all that sort of stuff," and "gorgeous geography lessons learning to weather forecast."

Rosalind worked hard in school and went to Cambridge University to study chemistry. World War II broke out during her second year there, and her father wanted her to help her country by volunteering on a farm. Rosalind contended she'd be more useful as a scientist—and she was right.

Working for the government, she pioneered the use of a technology called crystallography to reveal the molecular structure of coal, which was vital to the war effort—both as a source of power and as a component in gas masks. By the time Rosalind was twenty-five, she had written five papers about coal and earned her PhD. Even as German bombs were falling around her, she bicycled across London to the lab where she worked. Years later she admitted she had been terrified.

After the war, Rosalind took a job at King's College in London. There, she once again used crystallography to understand the structure of a substance. This time it was something much more complicated than coal; it was DNA (deoxyribonucleic acid), the molecule that transmits genetic information from a cell to its descendant.

Scientists already knew that DNA did this. What they didn't know was how.

No one had ever used crystallography to look at a material like DNA. The analysis required Rosalind's unique combination of know-how and persistence.

While Rosalind and her colleague, Maurice Wilkins, tried to unlock DNA's secrets, two scientists at Cambridge University were working on the same problem. Without Rosalind knowing it, they got hold of a summary of her data and one of her crystallographs, known as photo 51—the clearest image yet of DNA's structure. In 1957, the two Cambridge scientists—James Watson and Francis Crick—published a paper that accurately described the structure of DNA and how it worked.

Rosalind had been scooped!

It was many years before the public understood the extent of the injustice. Meanwhile, Rosalind had work to do. She went to another university lab and studied viruses, eventually learning how they use RNA (ribonucleic acid) to pass on genetic information. The work was critical to understanding infectious diseases and, more generally, molecular biology.

In 1962, James Watson, Francis Crick, and Maurice Wilkins shared the Nobel Prize for one of the most important discoveries of the twentieth century, the structure of DNA. Tragically, Rosalind wasn't around to see this. She died of ovarian cancer in 1958.

Rosalind believed it was important not only for scientists but for the public to understand science. One month before she passed away, she completed her final building project—a five-foot-tall model of a virus for display at the 1958 World's Fair in Brussels.

ROSALIND FRANKLIN

Achievement: Molecular biologist who uncovered the molecular structure of coal, living cells, and viruses. Her work on DNA made a key contribution to understanding how cells pass along traits, one of the most important discoveries in the history of science.

Quote: "Science and everyday life cannot and should not be separated."

Fascinating fact: As a teenager, Rosalind fell in love with all things French, especially French fashion. For the rest of her life, she liked to design and make her own clothes in the French style.

MARIE THARP

GEOLOGIST AND CARTOGRAPHER
1920-2006

A ROUND-FACED LITTLE GIRL with red curls is writing resolutions in her diary. One resolution is to faithfully keep the diary. Another is this: "Be as independent as possible."

The diary doesn't go so well. It stops after twelve entries. But decades later, Marie Tharp's resolute independence will help her stand up for her own ideas and change the way scientists think about the surface of the Earth.

As a child in the 1920s, Marie loved to join her dad at work. William Tharp was a soil surveyor, which means he made maps and tested soil samples to help farmers figure out how best to use land. On the job, William drove all over the countryside in a big truck. If Marie wasn't in school, she was riding shotgun beside him.

While Papa was busy, she made mud pies, drew pictures, or set up camp for her dolls in the rocks. Together they looked for arrowheads to add to his collection. When she was eleven, he taught her how to drive the truck.

Later Marie would say that because of those early expeditions, she had mapmaking in her blood.

Marie's dad was almost fifty when she was born, and her mom was over forty—old for parents in those days. Marie's half-brother lived elsewhere, and she grew up an only child. The family moved around a lot for her dad's job, and Marie attended more than fifteen schools before she graduated from high school. Always the new kid, she didn't have many friends, and became super close to her parents.

Not that she was a goodie-two-shoes. One time she came home from a school field trip and presented her mother with a burlap bag. Mom opened it and shrieked. The bag was full of snake skins and reptile skeletons.

When Marie was growing up, girls were expected to wear skirts or dresses to school. One freezing winter day in Cooperstown, New York, her parents sent Marie to school in ski pants. Unacceptable, said the principal. He sent her home and even gave her detention.

Marie knew this wasn't fair, but she accepted it. Likewise, she accepted the restrictions on her likely career—a secretary, a nurse, or a teacher. Few women had the chance to work outdoors like her dad did.

But then something big happened to change things: World War II. With men away at war, different jobs opened up for women. One of them was geologist—studying rocks and the Earth—similar to what her dad did. She earned a master's degree in geology and another in math.

She took a job as a geologist at an oil company, got bored, and took a job at a Columbia University lab in New York studying the ocean floor. The guys in the lab got to go out on research ships, but not Marie. This was in 1948, and some people—like Maurice Ewing, who ran the lab—thought women on ships were unlucky.

For several years, Marie's work was demanding but not that interesting. Change came in 1952 when a colleague named Bruce Heezen (pronounced HAY-zen) walked into her office with a whole lot of cardboard boxes full of scrolls. These were fathograms—printouts of ocean depth measurements collected over the previous five years by a ship-board instrument called a continuous echo sounder.

The sounder did three things: sent a ping sound to the bottom of the ocean; measured how long it took the echo of the ping to come back; and printed the results. In that way, it recorded the changing depth beneath the moving ship.

Marie's job was to take all those numbers, thousands and thousands of them, and translate them into drawings. In other words, she was making a relief map. No map like that of the ocean floor had ever been made, which meant that as she worked, Marie was revealing things that until then had been invisible. It had been suspected for a long time that there was a mountain range beneath the Atlantic Ocean. Marie's drawing confirmed this, and also revealed something new: There was a gully, or rift, that followed the ridge line of the mountain range.

Ever since maps of the world first appeared, people had noticed that the coastlines of the continents fit together like jigsaw puzzle pieces. In the early twentieth century a German geologist theorized that there had once been a single land mass that had split, with the pieces drifting apart over billions of years. This theory was called continental drift, and most scientists thought it was crazy.

But the rift Marie saw suggested maybe that idea wasn't crazy at all.

When she got additional data that showed undersea earthquakes tended to be centered along the rift, she became convinced. The forces that caused today's earthquakes had split the single continent right there. And inch by inch, those forces continued to move the continents.

Working together as much as they did, Bruce had become more than a colleague; he had become Marie's best friend. But when she told him what she suspected, even he thought she was wrong. This is where Marie's resolute independence came in. They fought about it—even threw things at each other—but she didn't back down. She kept working, kept collecting data, kept drawing maps. By the mid-1960s, Marie also gained a place on research ships.

Over the years, new exploration, eventually including photographs and precise measurements from satellites, yielded more information to back the theory of continental drift. Today it is well established as part of a larger explanation for the behavior of the surface of the Earth—plate tectonics.

Bruce died in 1977, and Marie retired from her job in 1982. At that time, a lot of people gave Bruce credit for work the two of them had done. But in the 1990s her contribution was recognized with awards from President Bill Clinton, the Library of Congress, and Columbia University.

Marie was not only a great scientist, she was a snappy dresser. Till the end of her life, she wore purple eyeliner and glitter nail polish. She had no patience for girly shoes, though. She favored Nike sneakers. And remember those arrowheads she collected with her dad? She made a necklace from them, and it was her favorite.

MARIE THARP

Achievement: Geologist and cartographer who made the first comprehensive map of the ocean floor, revealing a rift that substantiated the theory of continental drift, contributing to a more accurate understanding of the workings of planet Earth.

Quote: "As Papa always told me, 'When you find your life's work, make sure it is something you can do, and most important, something you like to do.'"

Fascinating fact: Marie owned a succession of big black poodles named Inky, after her friend Bruce's childhood dog. Her last poodle was white, but she named him Inky too.

VERA COOPER RUBIN

ASTROPHYSICIST

1928-2016

LYING ON THE BACK seat of the family car, the little girl stares up through the window at the sky. It's 1933, and seatbelts are in the future. Her dad is driving along a winding road at night, and the five-year-old notices something funny. Trees and telephone poles whiz by, but the moon seems to stick with her wherever she goes.

Why is that?

As it turns out, this particular girl will spend her life looking at the sky and asking questions. The question about the moon is reasonable. It seems to follow the car because it's very far away. Unlike the trees and poles, its position compared to the little girl barely changes.

On the other hand, some of the girl's questions will be as crazy as the one she thinks of next: Could she maybe redesign the sidewalks by her house so that some go only downhill and the others go only up? If she can figure out how to do this, she will use the downhill sidewalks. *I'm pretty lazy,* the girl admits to herself. *I don't like to trudge uphill.*

Vera Cooper's parents are used to her questions and do their best to answer. Still, nothing she thinks up as a child will be as strange as the real-life discovery that caps her career, the discovery that most of the matter in the universe is dark matter—not only invisible but undetectable.

Vera's family moved from Philadelphia to a new house in Washington, D.C., when she was ten. From her pillow, she looked north out her bedroom window at the stars. Soon she was hooked on the view. In fact, she found nothing else in her life as beautiful or as interesting.

In those days, the lights of the big city were not so very bright, and Vera regularly

saw meteor showers. Throughout the night, she would memorize the meteors' paths so that in the morning she could draw maps of their trails.

One time her mother, Rose, was going out for the evening and called upstairs to her daughter, "Vera! Don't spend the whole night with your head out the window!"

When she was thirteen, her father, Philip, an electrical engineer who had come to the United States from Lithuania, helped her build a telescope. Vera took the bus downtown by herself to obtain a cardboard tube. She ordered the lenses in the mail. Once the contraption was assembled, she tried to take photos through it, but that didn't work. Still, she wasn't discouraged. Building the telescope had been fun. And by this time, she knew she wanted to be an astronomer.

Always inspired by the view from her window, Vera went to the library and read books about the stars. In one she learned about a professor at Vassar College, Maria (pronounced Mar-EYE-ah) Mitchell, who had discovered a comet in the nineteenth century. With her in mind, Vera decided to attend Vassar too. She was excited when she was accepted and earned a scholarship. When she told her high school physics teacher—a macho kind of guy, she said later—he told her she would probably do okay, as long as she stayed away from science.

Ha! Vera graduated in three years with a degree in astronomy. Then, with her new husband, Robert, she went to Cornell University to study the motion of galaxies—giant clusters of stars, planets, and space dust that spin around a gravitational center. The Earth is located in the Milky Way Galaxy.

In November of 1950, Vera gave birth to a son. A month later, she traveled in a snowstorm to an academic conference to deliver a paper about her work. Her paper was called "Rotation of the Universe," a pretty ambitious title for a young person nobody knew. Most of the other astronomers at the conference thought Vera's work was nonsense. Some of them even said so.

This was discouraging, and for a while, Vera stayed home with her growing family while her husband worked as a physicist. Vera adored her children, but she had never expected that her husband would go off to work every day while she stayed home. She still subscribed to the *Journal of Astrophysics*. Every time a new issue arrived, she burst into tears. Finally, her husband insisted that she go back to school to earn her PhD, and, with help from her parents and from him, that's exactly what she did.

Looking back, Vera said her approach to astronomy was unusual because for a long time she was an outsider in the scientific community. She didn't know that certain things had already been decided or that other things were thought to be impossible. She just kept asking questions.

In the early 1970s, Vera and another astronomer, Kent Ford, were mapping the way mass—the scientific word for stuff—is laid out in galaxies. Once they had the mass figured out, they used an instrument called a spectrograph to learn how fast the contents of a galaxy were spinning. The laws of physics, as set out by Isaac Newton and Albert Einstein, among others, dictated that things at the edges of the galaxy should spin much more slowly than things in the middle, where the force of gravity is stronger.

But Vera and Kent's data showed that was wrong. In fact, the matter on the edges rotated at the same speed as what was in the middle. Vera and Kent studied one galaxy after another, hundreds of them, and the story was always the same. The galaxies should have been spinning apart, all the matter in them blasting out into space, but they weren't. What was holding them together?

The question was driving Vera crazy, and one day she decided she just had to know the answer. She took a pencil and a piece of paper and began making sketches. All of a sudden—she never knew why or how—the answer came to her. If a galaxy was surrounded by a huge amount of matter that she couldn't see and that her instruments couldn't detect, the gravitational pull of all that unseen matter would hold the visible part together.

The idea that there might be invisible matter in the universe wasn't new. A German astronomer had come up with it in the 1930s, but almost no one took it seriously. The implication was that scientists didn't even know what the universe was made of—a shocking suggestion. Now Vera and Kent had solid evidence that dark matter exists.

In the years since Vera and Kent's discovery, dark matter has become a generally accepted phenomenon and an important part of the explanation for how the universe began and grew. At the same time, competing theories have arisen. According to one proposed by physicist Erik Verlinde, our understanding of gravity itself must be revised. Change that, and dark matter is no longer necessary for explaining how the universe works.

Disagreements like this have been going on as long as humans have observed the Earth and the sky. Without debate, science would not progress.

Vera Cooper Rubin died in 2016. She spent both her childhood and her adulthood looking at the stars and asking questions. Looking at the Andromeda Galaxy, the one nearest to our own, she used to wonder whether some astronomer on a planet there might be looking out and observing us. "Always," she said, "I wished we could exchange views."

VERA COOPER RUBIN

Achievement: Astrophysicist who studied the rotation of galaxies with colleague Kent Ford, discovering substantial evidence for dark matter, now widely believed to make up most of the universe.

Quote: "In a spiral galaxy, the ratio of dark-to-light matter is about a factor of ten. That's probably a good number for the ratio of our ignorance to knowledge. We're out of kindergarten, but only in about third grade."

Fascinating fact: No woman had ever been allowed to use the telescope at the Mount Wilson observatory in California before Vera got there in the 1960s, and no women's restroom was available. So Vera took scissors, cut a skirt shape out of paper, and pasted it over the silhouette of a man on the door. "There," she said. "Now you have a women's restroom."

青蒿素

TU YOUYOU

PHARMACOLOGIST
BORN 1930

THE BANK MANAGER IS a big fan of poetry, especially the *Chinese Book of Odes*, compiled by the great philosopher Confucius. When the banker's only daughter is born, he insists on giving her an unusual name—Youyou. In one of the poems he loves, "youyou" is the glad sound a deer makes when it eats a certain yellow wildflower.

Most likely, the banker chooses the name because he thinks his new daughter is as sweet as that flower, and her birth makes him as happy as that deer. But the name turns out to have more significance. In fact, it's at the heart of an almost unbelievable coincidence.

In ancient China, the yellow wildflower, qinghao (pronounced ching-HOW), was believed to have healing powers. And four decades later, Tu Youyou—by then part of a top secret government program—would use it to make a lifesaving contribution to worldwide health.

Youyou grew up with her parents and four brothers in a house built by her grandfather in Ningbo, a 7,000-year-old port city on the east coast of China.

During Youyou's childhood, China endured civil war, Japanese invasion, and World War II. Fighting killed thousands of people. Hunger and disease killed more.

Her family was fortunate, and Youyou herself stayed safe. Her grandfather had been a college professor, and her parents believed education was important. They sent her to excellent schools. Then, when she was sixteen, she got sick with a terrible lung disease, tuberculosis, and had to take two years off.

The experience taught Youyou the value of good health. When she recovered, she decided she wanted to develop medicines for her own good and for others.

In 1951, Youyou left home for Beijing, the Chinese capital. There she took college courses at first and later worked and did research. She learned botany, biology, chemistry, and physiology. She also researched plant-based medicines and treatments used by traditional healers. Some of these treatments were thousands of years old.

During this same period, Youyou married a classmate from middle school, Li Tingzhao. The couple had two daughters.

Meanwhile, the political situation remained tough. In 1949, the communists, led by Mao Zedong, won the Chinese civil war and formed a government. After so many years of conflict, the country was very poor, and sometimes the leaders' plans to fix problems wound up making things worse.

In 1966, the government tried something new, a Cultural Revolution. It was supposed to create a society based on new principles. As a first step, Mao and the other leaders dictated that some old ideas had to go.

How did they try to get rid of these ideas?

By sending people who believed them, mostly well-educated people like scientists, away from their homes to camps in the countryside. The theory was that working alongside laborers in the fields would make these people better members of the new society.

Youyou's husband, Tingzhao, was sent to the countryside.

But Youyou was not.

Why?

This is where the top secret program comes in.

China was not only trying to set up a new society, it was also helping a neighboring country, North Vietnam, fight a war. One of North Vietnam's problems was soldiers getting sick and dying of malaria, a parasitic disease spread by mosquitoes. So the leaders of North Vietnam asked Mao's government to come up with a malaria treatment.

And Mao's government asked Youyou. At the time, she was working for the Academy of Traditional Chinese Medicine, and the government wanted someone with her expertise in specifically Chinese treatments.

Here is something else you should know about malaria: There is more than one kind. Some malaria can be cured with a drug that has been around for a long time, chloroquine. But some malaria is chloroquine-resistant. That's the kind Youyou wanted to treat.

Project 523 was named for May 23, 1967, the date it got off the ground. The government kept the project secret because it didn't want everyone to know it was helping North Vietnam, but also because it was sort of embarrassing. On one hand, leaders were sending scientists to the countryside because scientific ideas were considered out of place in the new society. On the other hand, the leaders were counting on scientists to solve a big health problem.

Youyou started by going to Hainan in southern China. Because of the hot, humid climate there, mosquitoes were plentiful and so was malaria.

Youyou had to leave her daughters—ages one and four—behind. Since her husband had been sent away, her parents came to take care of the baby. The four-year-old went to live with a teacher.

"The work was the top priority, so I was certainly willing to sacrifice my personal life," Youyou said later. In Hainan, "I saw a lot of children who were in the latest stages of malaria. Those kids died very quickly."

Within three months of starting her job, Youyou had identified and read about more than 2,000 potential treatments. From these, she chose 640 to test.

The work was very hard. Facilities were poor. Sometimes Youyou's team had to use kitchen pots instead of lab equipment. Sometimes fumes from toxic chemicals made them sick.

Qinghao, the wildflower in the poem that inspired her name, was one treatment they tested. To do so, they boiled the leaves and extracted a chemical from them. Then they tried the chemical out on mice whose blood had been contaminated with malaria parasites. When they examined blood samples, they saw that some of the parasites had been destroyed, but not all.

This was hopeful, so Youyou reread the traditional prescriptions. One was from a fourth-century scroll by a healer named Ge Hong. It didn't say anything about boiling qinghao. It said to soak the plant in cold water, wring out the leaves, and drink the juice.

Youyou tried this method, gave the new extract to the mice, and examined their blood. All of the malaria parasites were gone. Youyou and her team had extracted a medicine called artemisinin from a weed known in English as sweet wormwood. And the medicine worked!

Youyou is famously calm and soft-spoken. Many years later she looked back and said, "Of course, that was a really happy moment in my career as a researcher."

You might think such a big discovery would have been greeted with fireworks, celebration, and a huge prize.

But it wasn't. Not at first.

Youyou made a presentation to Chinese scientists in 1972 and later to world scientists. In 1976, the Cultural Revolution came to an end. Youyou's husband returned. Youyou went back to work. Family life resumed in the small apartment in Beijing.

For reasons having to do with world politics, artemisinin did not become part of the standard treatment for malaria worldwide until the early 2000s. Today it is credited with saving the lives of as many as 100,000 people each year.

In 2011, two American researchers, Louis Miller and Su Xinzhuan, dug into the history of the drug and learned about Youyou, who was still living in Beijing. Recognized at last, she won an American prize, the Lasker-DeBakey Award, for her discovery, and later the Nobel Prize for medicine.

"This honor belongs to me, my team, and the entire nation," she said at the Nobel ceremony.

Once the international community began recognizing Youyou, the Chinese government did too. Now her childhood home in Ningbo has been preserved as a historic site. Families visit often, and when they do, parents encourage their children to work hard and study science, just like Tu Youyou.

TU YOUYOU

Achievement: Pharmacologist who combined scientific testing methods with knowledge of traditional Chinese medicine to develop a lifesaving treatment for malaria.

Quote: "It is scientists' responsibility to continue fighting for the health care of all humans."

Fascinating fact: According to tradition, the ancient Chinese doctor Shen Nong tasted herbal treatments to make sure they were safe. In other words, he experimented on himself. Toward the end of their study for the government, Youyou and her team were in a hurry and did the same thing. Trying their own artemisinin extract for a week under doctors' supervision helped convince them it was safe.

SYLVIA EARLE

OCEANOGRAPHER

BORN 1935

*W*HAT WERE THOSE THINGS, anyway?

Brown, low-to-the-ground, and apparently armor-plated, they advanced on the beach like invading ankle-high army tanks. They seemed to be some kind of pointy-tailed crab, but they were awfully big—some almost the size of the kitchen sink at home.

Curious, the girl stared as they continued to come up onto the beach. Whatever they were, they were obviously ocean dwellers.

The poor things! What were they doing up here on the sand? For sure they would die if they stayed out of the water too long.

The girl couldn't let that happen.

So one by one, she picked them up and returned them to the sea.

In time, Sylvia Earle would find out her mistake. The mysterious creatures coming ashore in New Jersey were *Limulus polyphemus*, commonly called horseshoe crabs, recognized as living fossils because they so closely resemble their ancestors, which lived 450 million years ago.

And while Sylvia was right that they mostly live in the ocean, these guys didn't need help to get back to the water. The big females had come to the beach to lay their eggs and the smaller males to fertilize them. Over time, Sylvia would learn that horseshoe crabs can live forty years, that their eggs provide food for migrating sea birds, and that they have blue blood, vital for human vaccines.

Sylvia never forgot those horseshoe crabs. Eventually, she would devote her life to learning all she could about life in the ocean and doing everything in her power to protect it.

Until she was twelve, Sylvia lived with her mother, father, and brothers on a farm in

New Jersey. It was a pretty great life, and she knew it. Their rambling old house was built before the Revolutionary War. There were fruit trees, farm animals, and a pond. She even had a pony.

Sylvia's mom was trained as a nurse, but at heart she was a teacher. If Sylvia brought a snake into the house, her mom didn't say *yuck*. She admired its elegance and told Sylvia to be gentle because a snake is sensitive.

Sylvia was an independent child. Every chance she got, she set out alone to do what her mom called "investigations," observing the wild creatures—birds, frogs, and raccoons—that shared the farm with her family.

In Washington, D.C., a few years later, future physicist Shirley Ann Jackson (see page 67) would collect bees. On her farm, Sylvia had a greater variety of critters to observe and sometimes catch. Often she sat in the branches of a willow tree, observing wildlife and writing in her notebook.

In 1947, when Sylvia was twelve, her father announced that the family was moving to Florida. This was a shock! Sylvia loved the farm. She didn't want to go. But when the family arrived at their new house near Dunedin, she realized she had a whole new world to discover—a world that included saltwater marshes and the Gulf of Mexico.

For her birthday that year, she received a pair of goggles she could wear to see clearly while swimming or snorkeling. Now her investigations included the underwater world as well. Scuba diving was a pretty new thing when Sylvia learned at age sixteen.

To find out more about what she was seeing when she dove, she read the family's encyclopedia. At the local library, she found books by an explorer named William Beebe. In the 1930s, he and his friend Otis Barton had submerged themselves in the Atlantic Ocean off the coast of Bermuda in a bathysphere—a hollow, cast-iron ball just big enough for two people, with portholes, electric lights, and an oxygen tank.

Do you think teenage Sylvia suspected that one day she herself would design and operate equipment for underwater exploration? That's exactly what happened. Many years later, in 1982, she cofounded a company to do just that.

Sylvia went to college to study marine botany, began graduate studies, got married, and had children. In 1964, she joined the crew of a research vessel on a six-week voyage to study marine life in the western Indian Ocean. Being the only woman onboard didn't faze her. In college, she had often been the only woman in her science classes.

Sylvia earned her doctorate in 1966 with research on brown algae in the Gulf of Mexico. Brown algae may not sound thrilling, but Sylvia thought it was beautiful. One variety, sargassum, forms a vast canopy on the ocean that supports all kinds of animals and other plants. For her research, Sylvia collected 20,000 samples of algae, discovered many new varieties, and wrote the first of her twelve books.

In 1970, Sylvia was thirty-five years old and an accomplished scientist. Still, almost no one had ever heard of her. Then came Tektite II, an experimental underwater research station off the coast of St. John in the Caribbean Sea. Named for a glassy meteorite found on the ocean floor, Tektite I had an all-male crew. Tektite II's was all women, and Sylvia was its leader.

For two weeks, Sylvia and four teammates spent their days swimming in their new underwater neighborhood and their nights sleeping in a pressurized, enclosed habitat. The project, paid for by the National Aeronautics and Space Administration (NASA), was not only intended for ocean research but also to find out how people fared in a strange, isolated environment.

For Sylvia and the other scientists, the best part was becoming so familiar with the area that they recognized aquatic neighbors like eels and angel fish as individuals, not just members of a species.

Later she would say that spending two weeks underwater had changed her forever: "I wish that everyone could go and live underwater, if only for a day."

When Sylvia surfaced, she was surprised to discover she had become a celebrity. The city of Chicago threw the Tektite team a parade, and she was invited to lecture to big crowds. At first she was eager to return to her laboratory work, but then she realized she also had a duty to speak up for the ocean.

Since then, Sylvia's life has been full of science, exploration, and adventure. In 1979, she wore a big, heavy diving suit called a Jim to visit the floor of the Pacific Ocean near Hawaii. At a depth of 1,250 feet, deeper than anyone has traveled untethered in that kind of suit before or since, she walked among red crabs, orange fish, and glowing blue-green bamboo coral.

Over her long life, Sylvia has spent more than 8,000 hours undersea, diving in all five of the world's oceans—Pacific, Atlantic, Indian, Arctic, and Southern. One time, a blue shark came at her, and she kicked at it with her flippers to scare it away. Swimming with whales, she noted that their singing made her whole body vibrate.

In 2009, she founded Mission Blue, which works to set aside "hope spots," areas that are protected so that fish and other ocean wildlife can recover from over fishing and pollution. Sylvia likes to call these areas Giving Back Zones instead of No-Take Zones.

When Sylvia was three years old, a wave twice her height sent her tumbling. This was on one of her first trips to the beach. For a moment, she felt as if she couldn't breathe. But when the wave receded she found her footing.

Sylvia's mom was beside her and tried to haul Sylvia back to shore, but the little girl had other ideas. Like a fish, she wriggled away and jumped into the next wave. That day, she wrote later, the ocean won her heart.

SYLVIA EARLE

Achievement: Oceanographer who discovered new species, made record-setting dives, designed pioneering undersea exploration technologies, and founded Mission Blue to champion creation of marine sanctuaries worldwide.

Quote: "Far and away the greatest threat to the ocean and thus to ourselves is ignorance. But we can do something about that."

Fascinating fact: Queens are sometimes called "her highness." Since her record-setting dive in 1979, Sylvia's nickname has been "her deepness."

LYNN ALEXANDER MARGULIS

BIOLOGIST
1938-2011

SHE RUNS AWAY AT age thirteen, not from home but from school. Her algebra class is too hard. Who needs it?

Also, she has been at the same school since fourth grade. It's a very small school. She knows every single boy there as if they were her brothers; not one is boyfriend material.

The school she has been attending is a fancy one run by the University of Chicago. Convinced the nearby public school will be easier, she takes a bus there, finds the office, and enrolls.

For three months, everything goes according to plan. Then, just as her social possibilities are expanding, she is called into the principal's office.

We've asked your old school for your records, the principal explains. *There seems to be a problem.*

Busted, the girl's first reaction is to argue, but finally she admits the truth. She never told her old school she was leaving. She never told her parents either.

When her parents find out what she's been up to, there's a lot of crying, but in the end the girl gets to stay at the big public school. Two years later, she's bored. It turns out she misses the challenge of difficult classes, even algebra. So in 1954, at age fifteen, she takes a test that allows her to enroll early at the University of Chicago.

A little more than three years after that, she will graduate with a bachelor's degree in liberal arts, a husband, and a new interest in genetics.

Lynn Alexander grew up during the Depression of the 1930s in a tough Chicago neighborhood. Even in the city, she loved to be outdoors. When she was very small, she would lie on the ground and watch ants going about their business among the blades of grass. She wanted to understand them. Later she would say it always felt right to go into nature.

The man Lynn married at nineteen was the soon-to-be-famous astronomer Carl Sagan. The marriage lasted only seven years, but Carl had a big influence on his young wife, encouraging her to embark on a career in science. In Chicago, Wisconsin, California, and Massachusetts, Lynn studied *Euglena*, microscopic single-cell animals that live in freshwater and can feed like either an animal or a plant.

Lynn was living in Boston, a single mom with two sons and a poorly paid college teaching job at Boston University, when she wrote the paper that changed science. Having stared through microscopes for years, she knew that mitochondria—the energy-producing structures inside most living cells—looked a lot like bacteria. Other scientists had noticed this too, but most thought it was a coincidence.

Lynn's paper proposed another idea.

Mitochondria resembled bacteria because that's what their ancestors were. Billions of years ago, she theorized, two tiny bacteria living near each other had begun cooperating. Over time, the benefits of their cooperation caused them to merge, and from that merger evolved complex animals able to breathe oxygen, as well as complex plants able to convert sunlight to energy.

Most scientists thought cooperation had nothing to do with evolution. They believed evolution moved forward only because of competition. Organisms that did better at getting food and oxygen reproduced more, crowding out others. They were the winners because their offspring survived, and so did the useful traits that made them successful.

Lynn was not the first scientist to champion cooperation. A Russian named Peter Kropotkin had come up with a similar theory. Like Marie Tharp resurrecting continental drift or Vera Cooper Rubin discovering dark matter, Lynn had the courage and insight to consider the possibility that a crazy idea might be right.

The paper Lynn wrote in 1966 was rejected by fifteen scientific journals before one finally published it.

In 1970, Lynn wrote more about her theory in a book, *The Origin of Eukaryotic Cells*—the kind of cells that make up animals and plants. Some scientists ridiculed her. Some even attacked her. She did not back down. Later she would say she never considered her ideas controversial. She considered them right.

Finally, in 1978, new technology enabled scientists to analyze the DNA, or gene structure, of mitochondria. This analysis showed that mitochondrial DNA is different from that of the rest of the cell, which is convincing evidence that mitochondria had once been independent organisms—bacteria.

Elated, Lynn strode into the class she was teaching at the time, smiling and waving a copy of the study that backed her up.

Lynn believed one mistake her critics made was focusing on fossils of comparatively large creatures. Instead, they should have looked at the history of microbes like bacteria, which had been around for billions of years before trilobytes, dinosaurs, and people ever came along.

In 1967, Lynn married another scientist, Thomas Margulis. With him, she had two more children before once again divorcing. Later she would say she quit her job as a wife twice, finding it impossible to be a mother, a scientist, and a wife all at once.

In 1997, Lynn was named a distinguished professor of geoscience at the University of Massachusetts in the small town of Amherst. There she was a popular teacher. She rode her bicycle all over the place, dressed in colorful clothes, adopted rescue dogs, and filled her house with guests. In her lifetime, she wrote twenty books, some with her oldest son, Dorion Sagan.

She also embraced some pretty eccentric theories about disease and even about government. Some of her colleagues in science thought she enjoyed being outrageous and at the center of controversy.

Lynn's mother, Leona, had died young after suffering a stroke. Lynn always feared that she, too, would die young. According to Dorion, she lived her life to the fullest because she had so much to get done.

LYNN ALEXANDER MARGULIS

Achievement: Biologist who recognized that parts of cells, such as mitochondria (in animals) and chloroplasts (in plants), evolved from what were once independent bacteria, changing the way both cells and evolution are understood.

Quote: "There are hundreds of ways your body wouldn't work without bacteria. Between your toes is a jungle; under your arms is a jungle. . . . We take for granted their influence. They are our ancestors."

Fascinating fact: Having grown up during bad economic times, Lynn was careful with money and didn't like to waste anything. Her son once caught her eating a bowl of cut-up hot dogs mixed with breakfast cereal that her Irish wolfhound had turned down.

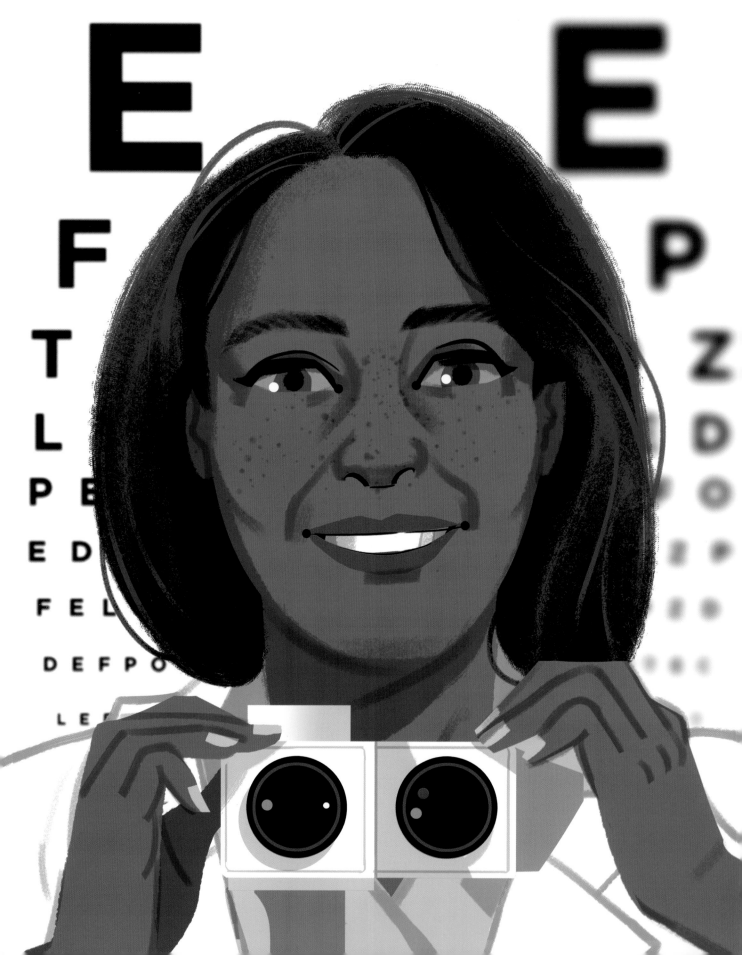

PATRICIA ERA BATH
PHYSICIAN AND INVENTOR
BORN 1942

THE LITTLE GIRL READS the newspaper every day. It's important to know what's going on in the world, she believes—maybe not as important as homework, but right up there. She shares this conviction with her dad. He drives a subway now, but before settling down in New York City he sailed the world with the merchant marine. Born on the island nation of Trinidad, he loves to talk about the places he's been, and his daughter loves to listen.

One day, reading the newspaper as usual, the girl sees a story about a doctor whose clinic in the African city of Lambaréné (now in Gabon) treats people with scary diseases like leprosy. The doctor's name is Albert Schweitzer. *I want to help people like he does,* she thinks.

When she tells her parents, they are all over it. The family doesn't have a lot of money, but Rupert and Gladys Bath believe "With an education, you can own the world." They give their daughter, Patricia, a microscope and later a chemistry set. When they tell her never to settle for less than her best, she promises she won't. Many years later, as a professor of medicine, she will follow Albert Schweitzer's example by developing innovations that prevent blindness and treat eye disease all over the world.

Patricia Bath grew up in the New York City neighborhood of Harlem in the 1940s and '50s. Like her parents, most of the neighbors were black and worked hard for very little money. The schools weren't the best. But looking back, Patricia saw the neighborhood as a source of happy memories. She didn't know any women doctors, but her own family doctor—a man—encouraged her in her career. Meanwhile, her parents taught her that being rich didn't mean having a lot of stuff; it meant being close to your family, being self-reliant, and learning. In that sense, Patricia grew up rich.

When she was sixteen, Patricia earned a spot doing cancer research in a prestigious summer program at Yeshiva University. Twenty-eight students from all over the city participated. A photo of Patricia presenting her research appeared on the front page of the *New York Times*.

As she spoke, another student raised his hand and tried to correct something she had just said. "Don't you mean that cancer is an anabolic rather than a catabolic process?"

"That's a common misconception," she replied calmly. "A growing tumor is a symptom of cancer, which is really a wasting, catabolic disease."

Patricia and her parents were thrilled when her research contributed to a study published by one of her professors.

Patricia graduated from high school in only three years and got a scholarship to study chemistry at Hunter College. After that, following in Dr. Schweitzer's footsteps, she headed to medical school at Howard University in Washington, D.C. To help pay the expenses, her mother worked as a house cleaner. "So that I could go to medical school, my mother scrubbed floors," Patricia later said.

Patricia chose eye health, ophthalmology, as her specialty. When she graduated in 1968, she worked in two New York City hospitals, one in Harlem and one in a more affluent neighborhood. Right away she noticed that her poorer patients were much more likely to have eye problems. When she did a study to find out more, she learned that people in Harlem were twice as likely to be blind as people in other parts of the city. Why was this? Patricia concluded that poorer people didn't get good eye care.

Dr. Schweitzer's mission was to cure leprosy. Dr. Bath's was to prevent blindness. With help from colleagues, she founded the American Institute for the Prevention of Blindness (AIPB), whose goal is to protect, preserve, and restore sight. She also pioneered community outreach programs, using volunteers to make good eye care and blindness prevention available to more people. Today this effort has saved the sight of tens of thousands of people all over the world.

In the 1980s, Patricia was a professor in Los Angeles when she came up with a novel idea. Cataracts, cloudy films that develop in the lens of the eye over time, are common causes of blurred vision and blindness. For decades, cataracts had been treated with a specialized drill that literally ground them up. But Patricia thought lasers—highly focused beams of light—might do a better job. Lasers would vaporize the film, so an artificial lens could be inserted in the eye. The lasers would also be less painful than the traditional method, and less likely to cause unintentional damage.

Few people agreed that this was a workable idea. In the United States at that time, lasers were more often used for military than medical purposes. So Patricia went to Germany, where laser research was more advanced, and spent five years working on perfecting her device. When at last it worked the way she wanted it to, she was so excited she didn't want to leave the lab.

Patricia patented her invention, the Laserphaco Probe, in 1988. Today laser surgery is a standard treatment for cataracts.

Like her inspiration, Dr. Schweitzer, Patricia eventually found her way to Africa. On a volunteer trip with AIPB, she operated on a woman who had been blind for thirty years. The procedure she performed, keratoprosthesis, replaces a diseased cornea—the transparent front part of the eye—with an artificial one. It worked like a charm. Patricia has received many awards and accolades over the years, but in the end she counts that achievement as her finest hour. "The ability to restore sight is the ultimate reward," she said.

PATRICIA ERA BATH

Achievement: Physician who invented a device that uses lasers to remove cataracts from the eyes; also pioneered community ophthalmology, which brings eye care and blindness prevention to underserved populations.

Quote: "Do not allow your mind to be imprisoned by majority thinking. Remember that the limits of science are not the limits of your imagination."

Fascinating fact: The first woman faculty member in ophthalmology at UCLA, Patricia refused to accept the office she was offered. It was in the basement next to the room that housed the lab animals. "I didn't say it was racist or sexist," she recalled later. "I said it was inappropriate." The administration gave her a better office.

CHRISTIANE NUSSLEIN-VOLHARD

BIOLOGIST

BORN 1942

THE GIRL WITH THE dark blond braids has been kneeling in the garden so long that her knees have got to hurt. If they do, she doesn't notice. She wants to know everything there is to know about that flower. By looking long enough and hard enough, she is convinced she will learn its deepest secrets.

Christiane, known as Janni (pronounced YANN-ee), is eight years old, and the garden is beside her family's apartment in Magdeburg, near the big city of Frankfurt, Germany.

When Janni was a toddler, Germany surrendered to the Allies, ending World War II in Europe. Even now, years later, the war's effects linger, and the family doesn't have much money.

Instead of doing without, kids and parents do it themselves. They make their own puzzles by gluing prints of famous paintings onto wood and then cutting out pieces with a jigsaw. They make their own clothes, write and illustrate their own books, play musical instruments after dinner, and sing.

Janni plays the flute and sings enthusiastically. One time she sings an opera solo so loudly that a neighbor comes over to complain.

Decades later, Christiane Nusslein-Volhard will credit her parents' do-it-yourself practicality and her own native curiosity for enabling the hard work that earned her a share of the 1995 Nobel Prize in medicine. That achievement was also the result of close examination, but this time Janni wasn't looking at flowers. She was looking at something even more unlikely.

Growing up, Janni was smart and curious but her grades were nothing special. If something bored her, like English class, she stopped paying attention. On the other hand, if she was interested in something, she attacked it with the same enthusiasm she showed for singing.

Janni attended college in Frankfurt then left home to study in the medieval town of Tübingen. There she lived in a house that was hundreds of years old and very charming, although it lacked comforts like hot water and central heat. Janni didn't mind. All her friends lived the same way, and there was an excellent movie theater right across the street.

Along about this time, she got married and divorced. Since her first scientific papers listed her as Christiane Nusslein-Volhard, she kept the name Nusslein even after the marriage ended.

Meanwhile, she was studying the latest developments in genetics—how living things inherit traits from their parents. To earn her doctorate, she studied RNA (ribonucleic acid), the molecule in bacteria that transmits genetic information.

Janni might have kept on looking at molecules, but she was—guess what—bored and wanted a new challenge. The one she took on was big, one of the most import- ant questions in biology: How does one cell develop into a complex organism? Janni knew she would need help answering this question, so she got some assistants— hundreds of thousands of them. These were *Drosophila melanogaster*, also known as red-eyed fruit flies.

You might think no one cares about fruit flies, but in fact they are important to scien- tific research. Why? Because they are tough, have a lot of offspring fast, and don't take up a lot of space in a lab. More importantly, they use the same basic chemical processes as people and every other animal to breathe, eat, grow, and move. Understanding how these processes work in fruit flies tells you something about how they work in other creatures, too.

For Janni's research, the important thing fruit flies have in common with other crea- tures is how they develop. They begin life as a single fertilized egg cell, but that cell divides to form new ones, which divide again, and so on. At first, the cells are nearly identical, but they change as they divide, transforming into the building blocks of nerves, bone, heart, skin, and every other part of the body.

When Janni began her research in 1975 it was known that genes direct cell development, but how did that work exactly?

To find out, Janni and her colleagues, including Eric Wieschaus, bred a whole lot of fruit flies—more than 40,000 families. In each family, they used chemical methods to remove one single gene, then they looked at the resulting embryos to see how they had been affected. For example, if the fly embryos had not developed a head, then the missing gene must regulate development of a head.

The work required long hours of staring at fruit fly embryos under a microscope, but Janni did not get bored. Like the flowers of her childhood, the fruit flies were beautiful to Janni because they were part of nature. Every morning when she came to work, she was excited. Maybe this would be one of those days when the microscope revealed some exciting change that had appeared overnight.

In the end, Janni and Eric's research led to many surprising conclusions. First, only 120 of the fruit fly's 20,000 genes were in charge of dictating the normal development of the embryo. Second, many of those genes were similar to those that cause genetic diseases in humans. Finally, the basic features of body organization are the same whether you're a fruit fly, a shark, a tarantula, or a person. This finding implies that all these body plans originated with a common ancestor.

In 1986, Janni wanted to see how her research applied to other creatures, specifically ones with backbones like fish, birds, reptiles, and mammals. Zebra fish embryos are transparent, making them easy to study, so Janni bought a few from a pet store. By 1993, she had 6,000 tanks and 100,000 fish.

She also had that Nobel Prize, shared with Eric and another American geneticist, Edward B. Lewis.

As of this writing, Janni is a director at the Max Planck Institute in Tübingen, Germany. She is serious about science and about other things, too. Long into adulthood, she played music with her brothers and sisters, skied, reads mystery novels, cooked for friends, and swam in the pond behind her house. But no matter what she does, she is precise about it. A friend once reported that if she invites you over to bake Christmas cookies, you'd better be sure the points on your stars are straight.

CHRISTIANE NUSSLEIN-VOLHARD

Achievement: Biologist who explained how genes regulate the development of single cells into complex animals, including people, providing unexpected insights into how the immune system fights off infectious diseases.

Quote: "Although the work we did was often tedious and sometimes frustrating, it was generally great fun and a deep pleasure and joy to get an understanding of what seemed initially to be a great mystery."

Fascinating fact: Channeling her do-it-yourself childhood, Janni designed and built housing for fruit flies and for zebra fish that have since been adopted for use by labs all over the world.

JOCELYN BELL BURNELL

ASTRONOMER

BORN 1943

IT'S THE FIRST DAY of school, and all the kids head off to science class—girls to one room, boys to another. Almost as soon as she gets settled at her desk, one girl suspects something is not right. The teacher is talking about household tasks. If this is science, it isn't the kind that she wants to do.

"I think I'm in the wrong place," she tells the teacher.

The teacher assures her she's in the right place. She's a girl, after all. And not only that, she failed the exam that determines whether students are bright enough to go to college. Supposedly, students like her are best suited for "domestic science," the very class she is in.

The girl's parents complain, and the next day she is allowed to join two other girls in a room full of boys in the lab science class. As it turns out, she is pretty good at science. In fact, as an astrophysics graduate student a little more than a decade later, Jocelyn Bell will discover a whole new kind of star, a finding that helps revolutionize the way we understand the universe.

Jocelyn Bell Burnell grew up in a big house near a small town in Armagh, Northern Ireland. The house was so remote that electricity was iffy. There was no vacuum cleaner or television; sometimes the lights went out. During World War II, when Jocelyn was a baby, sixteen adults lived there. Besides her own family, these included refugees from Adolf Hitler's Germany. The staff included a nanny, a cook, a maid, and a handyman.

Jocelyn's father, Philip, was an architect. From a young age, she shared his interest in building and made elaborate towns and structures for her dolls using Meccano building sets, which are still popular in Britain.

Jocelyn was also a great reader and often borrowed her father's books. Two favorites

were about astronomy. She didn't understand everything she read, but what she later called the "scale and splendor of the cosmos" fascinated her.

As a teenager, Jocelyn sometimes helped her father when he worked designing the Armagh Planetarium. The staff there were encouraging when she told them she might want to study astronomy someday, but one astronomer pointed out that part of the job was staying up all night to look at the sky.

Uh-oh, Jocelyn thought. She had always been the type who needed her sleep. She was sad for a while, thinking her career was done before it ever got started. Then she learned that some astronomers were using a new method in their work. Instead of looking at light coming from stars and other objects, they looked at data printouts of radio waves coming from them. This study required a special kind of telescope, but it did not require darkness.

After earning a university degree in physics in Scotland, Jocelyn went to Cambridge University in England to study quasars—very bright objects much larger than stars that are located billions of light years away. But before she could do her study, she had to help build a radio telescope.

Most people think of a tube you look through when they think of a telescope. But a radio telescope is actually a giant antenna. The one Jocelyn helped build was made up of a thousand poles strung with a hundred miles of wire and stretched over an area as big as four American football fields.

Besides building and studying, Jocelyn played field hockey. Hammering posts into the ground is an excellent workout, and soon she could hit the ball corner to corner, farther than anyone else on her team.

Building the telescope took two years. After it was powered up in July 1967, Jocelyn studied the data printouts—squiggly lines that represented electromagnetic signals given off by the stars and sensed by the telescope. The telescope spit out one hundred feet of paper a day. No matter how long Jocelyn worked, there were always printouts waiting.

At first, Jocelyn's big discovery didn't look big at all. It was a quarter-inch pattern in the midst of all those squiggles on all those yards of paper. But this pattern looked different. Jocelyn called it "scruff," Irish slang for a mess.

No one knew what made the electromagnetic waves that created the pattern. The source was way too small to be a star, let alone a quasar, but it was emitting a lot of energy.

Jocelyn's adviser, Antony Hewish, half joked that the source might be an alien civilization. For a while, he even called it "little green men." Jocelyn herself worried the cause might be a problem with the wiring of the telescope. Had she done something wrong?

Late one night in December, Jocelyn was reviewing printouts at her office at the university when she spotted a new "bit of scruff" in the data. This time the origin seemed to be in a part of the sky that would pass over the telescope at one a.m.

So much for finding a job in astronomy that would let her get her sleep.

With no time to spare, she jumped on her motor scooter and rode from her office out to the telescope. It was so cold that the equipment wasn't working right. Neither were Jocelyn's stiff fingers. Her feet were frozen. With a few swift kicks and her own hot breath, she got the receiver working. Studying the printout, she saw the pattern again.

Now she knew the first data didn't result from bad wiring. Whatever it was, there were two of them somewhere out there in the universe—new objects with properties that were totally unexpected. Over the next few months, Jocelyn found still more.

Since the radio waves appeared to come from these objects in pulses, the press invented the word "pulsar." More study revealed them to be spinning collapsed stars. Compared to other stars, they were tiny, with a diameter of only about ten miles. But their mass was millions of times larger, making them incredibly dense. A teaspoon of their substance would weigh one billion tons!

Six years later, in 1974, Antony Hewish and Martin Ryle won the Nobel Prize in physics based, in part, on the discovery of the pulsar. Jocelyn did not share the prize—something many people thought was unfair. Fred Hoyle, one of England's best-known astronomers, wrote that the achievement was only possible because Jocelyn had been willing "to contemplate as a serious possibility a phenomenon that all past experience suggested was impossible."

In 1968, Jocelyn earned her doctoral degree and married Martin Burnell. After that she taught and did research part-time at several different universities while taking primary responsibility for keeping house and raising her son—who grew up to be a physicist. Later, she and Martin divorced.

In 1991, Jocelyn became a full professor of physics, one of two women physics professors in Britain at the time. By then she had begun to receive recognition for her work as a physicist, a leader, an educator, and an advocate for women. In 2007, Queen Elizabeth II gave her the honor Dame Commander of the British Empire.

JOCELYN BELL BURNELL

Achievement: Astronomer who discovered the small, fast-spinning, neutron stars known as pulsars, the existence of which was entirely unexpected. The discovery led to new understanding of how stars live and die, super-dense matter, magnetic fields, general relativity, and gravity.

Quote: "I think the thing that surprises people most [about me] is that I am religious. I'm an elder in my church, which is the Quakers, or The Religious Society of Friends. A lot of people think that scientists aren't religious. It's not true."

Fascinating fact: Jocelyn was the only woman majoring in physics at the University of Glasgow in the early 1960s. Every time she entered a lecture hall her fellow students—all boys—stomped, hooted, and whistled. After a while, she taught herself not to blush.

$= \lim_{h \to 0} \frac{6h + h^2}{h}$
$= \lim_{h \to 0} (6 + h)$
$= 6$
$\frac{d}{dx}(au) = a\frac{du}{dx}$
$\frac{d}{dx}\log_a u = \frac{\log_a e}{u}\frac{du}{dx}$
$\frac{d}{dx}a^u = a^u \ln a \frac{du}{dx}$

SHIRLEY ANN JACKSON
PHYSICIST AND EDUCATOR
BORN 1946

MOST OF THE KIDS in the first-grade reading circle at Parkview Elementary in Washington, D.C., are well-behaved. They sit quietly until the teacher asks a question, then raise their hands and wait to be called on.

But there's always a troublemaker, right? In this class, the teacher has had to punish one girl by asking her to leave the circle. Not that it does any good. From her seat in the corner, the girl still calls out answers before anyone else has a chance. Her name is Shirley Ann Jackson, but her classmates call her Brainiac.

The teacher phones Shirley's mother, Beatrice, who offers some advice: Give Shirley a challenge. She needs to be working hard.

Beatrice is a smart woman. Soon Shirley is exceling at school. Years later, when she's in high school, Shirley will join the quiz bowl team and earn points instead of punishment for calling out answers first.

When Shirley was in first grade, schools were still segregated. In other words, white children and black children had to attend different schools. Not until she was in third grade would a famous court case, *Brown v. Board of Education*, bring about integration so that Shirley, who is African-American, can attend Barnard School, only three blocks from her house on Farragut Avenue.

Growing up, Shirley was not just brainy; she liked thrills and working with her hands. Her father, George, a decorated veteran of World War II, had never finished high school, but he was a math whiz and a born mechanic. With him, Shirley and her sister, Gloria, built soapbox cars out of spare parts scrounged from the neighborhood. Shirley called the cars hot rods but they were more like sleds on wheels. Building them was fun, and so was racing them—especially when she won.

Shirley had another outlet for her brains and daring—an unlikely one. Curious about insect behavior, she trapped bees in jars and kept them on a shelf under the porch. Shirley fed them different foods to see what they liked and learned that they got sleepy in the dark. Already a good scientist, she logged her observations faithfully.

Shirley's parents were strict, and their household was well-organized. Along with her three siblings, she always had chores to do: cleaning the bathroom, caring for the roses and the lawn, making the Saturday dinner of pork and beans. Shirley kept her own life well-ordered, too. On long summer days, she made a routine: swim lessons in the morning, bike to the library, check out the maximum five books, then spend the afternoon in the cool basement drinking Kool-Aid, eating crackers, and reading.

Shirley enrolled at the Massachusetts Institute of Technology (MIT) in 1964, one of the first women to attend the prestigious school, and one of only two black women. To her surprise, the white students seemed unfriendly. When, after a couple of months, she mustered her courage and asked to study with the girls on her hallway, they told her to go away.

Shirley cried, but she didn't quit. She had worked too hard to get to MIT, and she knew her parents and teachers had worked hard to help her. Four years later, as a graduate student, she remembered how lonely she had been. To make the college experience better for others, she established a chapter of the Black Student Union and led a task force on educational opportunity. Recruiting new students, she met smart kids whose high schools didn't offer enough math and science, so she helped create a program at MIT to get them ready for first-year classes.

At the same time, Shirley was taking classes herself and eventually doing the research into theoretical physics that would earn her a PhD. Early on, she applied for a summer job in the lab of a professor whose class she had aced. During the interview he asked if she could cook, and she was confused. Was he insulting her? Did he think she was applying for a job in the kitchen?

No, he didn't. He understood what job she wanted. He just believed that the skills required for cooking—including care and patience—overlapped those required in a lab.

He gave her the job, and it turned out to be tough. She was working with semiconductors, materials that today form the basis for electronic devices because of the way they conduct electricity. In the lab, Shirley had to create two metal alloys (mixtures of metals), layer them together, and test the result. Just as she had with the bees long before, Shirley had to keep careful records.

But do you know what? She was the same person she had always been. To stay happy—and well-behaved—she needed a challenge. She needed to be working hard.

In graduate school, Shirley focused on theoretical physics, using math to understand the behavior of materials like atoms and subatomic particles. In 1973, she became the first African-American woman to earn a PhD in that subject, and the first African American to earn a PhD at MIT.

As it turned out, Shirley's dual dedication to science and education while at MIT also defined her life's work. First she studied the behavior of subatomic particles—particles that are smaller than atoms—at research labs in the United States and Europe. Eventually she went to Bell Labs in New Jersey, where her theoretical work on semiconductors, much of it accomplished with pencil and paper, laid the groundwork for advances in phones, computers, televisions, and other devices.

In the 1990s Shirley became a physics professor at Rutgers University and then chair of the Nuclear Regulatory Commission, which helps ensure that nuclear power in the United States is safe. In 1999, she accepted a job as president of the Rensselaer Polytechnic Institute (RPI). As of this writing, the first-grade troublemaker is not only a theoretical physicist, but the president of a major American university.

SHIRLEY ANN JACKSON

Achievement: Physicist and educator who laid the groundwork for important advances in electronics through theoretical research into semiconductors, and continues to shape government, education, and public policy in science and science education.

Quote: "You cannot even aspire to be a scientist, engineer, entrepreneur, or technological leader until you are comfortable with calculus. And you can't begin to think about calculus unless you've mastered algebra. And before that multiplication, and before that addition and subtraction."

Fascinating fact: When an MIT professor told her that as a "colored woman," she should learn a trade, she told him that she already had. Her trade was physics.

INGRID DAUBECHIES

PHYSICIST AND MATHEMATICIAN
BORN 1954

THE GIRL IS MAKING a dress for one of her dolls. It is a painstaking process. She measures the doll. She draws a pattern just right to fit her. She cuts out the pattern, pins it to fabric, then cuts the fabric. At last she sews the seams, the facings, and the hem.

The girl likes making doll clothes because she likes solving problems. In this case, she thinks it's interesting that she has taken something two-dimensional, the flat piece of fabric, and made it three-dimensional to fit her doll.

Now she dresses her doll and admires her work. The doll really does look nice, ready for a party! The little girl is happy—elated even, but only for a few minutes.

Now that she has understood how to make the dress, maybe it isn't so special after all. Anyway, it's time for a new challenge. There is always another problem to solve, something to work on next.

The girl's ability to see the math in real-world problems—like making doll clothes—will one day make her a celebrated mathematician and physicist. But decades later when her own daughter, Carolyn, is diagnosed with attention deficit disorder (ADD), Ingrid Daubechies will note how she herself is always shifting focus from one thing to another.

Maybe she also has a mild form of ADD? If so, she tells her daughter, it isn't necessarily so bad.

Ingrid Daubechies grew up in Houthalen, a coal mining town in the Dutch-speaking part of Belgium. Ingrid's grandfather was so poor as a child that he quit school at nine to go to work in a glass factory. By the time he was fourteen, he had lost both an eye and a finger on the job.

Ingrid's father, Marcel, wanted to do better, so he went to college and became a mining engineer. Ingrid's mother, Simonne, stayed home to raise Ingrid and her brother.

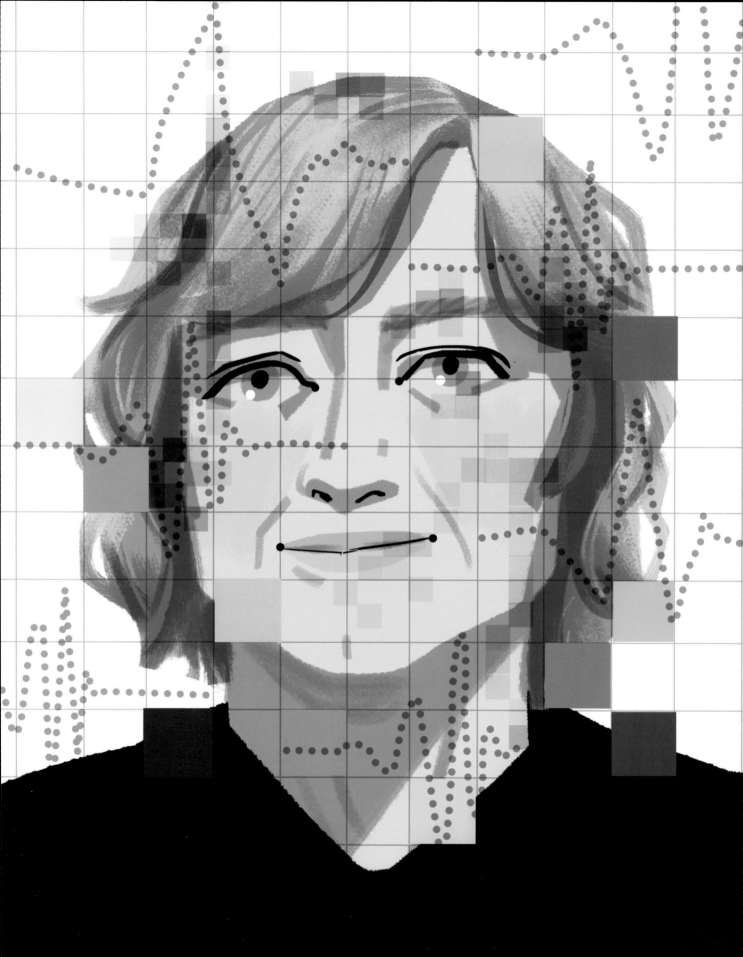

She also had a college degree. When her kids were grown, she went back to school for a master's degree in criminology and became a social worker.

Ingrid's father thought being an engineer was okay, but in college he had discovered his true love, physics. Ingrid liked to learn, and she liked her father—so when she was little she asked him questions about physics. Even when his answers went on a little too long, she tried to pay attention.

Later, she had children of her own who also asked questions. She tried to keep her answers brief.

As a child, Ingrid liked to make pots and to weave. She also studied machines to see how they worked. For fun, she thought about numbers. Did you know that when a number is divisible by nine, if you add all its digits together, you get another number divisible by nine?

Twenty-seven is an example. Multiplying nine times three is twenty-seven, so it is indeed divisible by nine. And the two digits, two and seven, add up to nine. Ingrid tried to figure out why this is so.

Many years later, when Ingrid met her future husband, Robert Calderbank, she immediately had a feeling they were going to get along. Like her, he had lulled himself to sleep as a child by doubling numbers in his head—one, two, four, eight, sixteen, thirty-two . . . and so on.

Ingrid went to college and graduate school in Belgium, then worked as a researcher. In 1988, she published a paper explaining the math that she is still best-known for, the Daubechies wavelet, which has transformed technologies used every day.

The wavelets Ingrid was talking about are like the ones in the ocean, but their spacing is perfectly even, and they don't have to be made of water. They could be light, or electrical energy, or even gravity. For years, electrical engineers had been using sub-band filtering, a concept related to wavelets, as a way to translate electrical signals. What Ingrid did was use mathematics to devise a new and better way to take apart a signal and convert it into pieces that could be worked with or stored.

Today the FBI relies on Daubechies wavelets to store the 200 million fingerprint images it has in its database, and sound engineers use them to eliminate unwanted noise from old recordings. Anyone taking a photo with a digital camera or phone is relying on these advanced mathematical tools, too.

What does math have to do with pictures?

Imagine a picture as a mosaic composed of many tiny pieces. In a digital image, those pieces are called pixels, and each has its own color and brightness. You could assign a number to each pixel according to color and brightness, then describe the picture as a series of those numbers. But that would be a lot of numbers!

Wavelet theory takes advantage of the fact that most pixels in a picture are similar to the ones nearby. What makes the picture a picture instead of a blob are the areas where there are big differences between one pixel and its neighbors.

Daubechies wavelets make it possible to store only the parts of the picture where big variations occur, while tossing out the parts where details are unnecessary. This is the basis of image compression.

The same idea can be used to restore old paintings. Working with a digital photograph of a medieval painting from a church in Belgium, Ingrid and her students mapped the location of cracks and virtually filled them in. This process made it easier for experts in medieval manuscripts to read some tiny words on a painted page that appears in the picture.

Using math as a way to apply an idea from electrical engineering more broadly is creative and original. But Ingrid doesn't necessarily think of herself as a genius. Instead, she believes she is good at bringing people and ideas together, stirring them up, and applying hard work and hard thinking to the results.

In 1987 Ingrid moved to the United States, so that she and her then-new husband, Robert, could live together. Like Shirley Ann Jackson (see page 67), Ingrid worked at Bell Labs, then became a professor.

When Ingrid was president of the International Mathematics Union, the first woman to hold the post, she promoted math education around the world, especially for women. She also cofounded a math workshop for high school-age girls at Duke University in North Carolina.

One of the many prizes Ingrid has won for her work came with $200,000, which she used to help her son, who teaches high school math on the south side of Chicago—a poor area. Since then, she has systematically set aside a portion of her prizes to help improve math education in developing countries.

Ingrid is a teacher as well as a researcher. One thing she tells students is that doing original research means you will fail a lot of the time. And since you're going to fail, you should celebrate extra hard when you have a success.

After that, she says, double check your results, and get back to work. Whether it's making doll clothes or figuring out how to restore an old painting, there is always a new challenge to look forward to.

INGRID DAUBECHIES

Achievement: Physicist and mathematician who developed wavelet theory, which revolutionized audio and visual processing, medical imaging, seismology, and surveillance, among many other technologies. As president of the International Mathematics Union, implemented innovative initiatives to support teaching math around the world.

Quote: "I think it must be a very rare person who does not feel insecure, like a whole assembly of failures with the occasional good thing in between. But realizing that everybody feels that way helps."

Fascinating fact: Ingrid did not grow up to be a princess. But she did grow up to be a baroness. For her outstanding contribution to mathematics and technology, King Albert II of Belgium honored her with that title in 2012.

ADRIANA OCAMPO

GEOLOGIST
BORN 1955

BORN IN COLOMBIA AND raised in Argentina, she is fourteen when her family moves to Southern California. She doesn't speak English, and she doesn't know a whole lot about the United States.

But she knows one thing. In fact, she has dreamed about it her whole life. She has barely stepped off the airplane when she asks, "Donde está NASA?"

One of three sisters, Adriana Ocampo fell in love with the points of light in the night sky when she was a very young child. Often she would play on the roof of her house with her fox terrier, Tauro. She hung up a sheet to make a tent that served as a space capsule, then created a space helmet out of an upside-down pot from the kitchen. Her only doll, a gift from her godfather, came wearing a tartan plaid outfit. Adriana covered it up with a space suit made of tin foil. She wanted her doll to be an astronaut too.

Adriana's mother was a teacher and her father an electrician. In Buenos Aires, Adriana learned to repair radios in her father's workshop. Her own family didn't have a car, but she tested her mechanical skills on her uncle's 1955 Oldsmobile.

In 1969, Adriana watched Neil Armstrong's historic moon landing on the only TV in her neighborhood. Other people marveled at the spacecraft or the space suit or the danger, but Adriana focused on the dirt and rocks beneath the astronaut's boots.

By this time, Adriana had decided she wanted to be a scientist and travel to space. Her teachers in Buenos Aires had told her she was better suited to business classes, but at her California high school she studied calculus and physics, then took science classes at Pasadena City College. Math was hard, but one of her teachers was especially tough and wouldn't let her quit. With a lot of work, she finally caught on.

Adriana did not find NASA the day she arrived in the United States. But it didn't take long. Still in high school, she began volunteering at the Jet Propulsion Lab (JPL), a division of NASA in Pasadena, California, not far from her family's home.

The first time she visited JPL was for volunteer orientation. Hanging from the ceiling of the auditorium was a satellite, and Adriana was thrilled. "¿Cómo funciona?" she asked. "How does it work?"

After Adriana graduated from high school, she was offered a job at JPL. For her, this was heaven. She was earning money to learn about what she loved! Forty years later she would still be at NASA, by this time directing missions that gather clues about the geology and formation of asteroids, comets, the Earth and other planets, and the solar system itself.

As a young adult, Adriana worked full time and went to university, eventually earning degrees in geology and planetary geology. In 1976, NASA chose her to be part of the team working on the Viking mission to Mars. Since her job was to help translate computer code transmissions from space into images, she was one of the first humans to see the surface of a Martian moon, Phobos.

For a later mission, Mars Observer, Adriana helped test and develop a thermal spectrometer, a device to collect information about the surface of Mars and its atmosphere. Unfortunately, the spectrometer never got the chance to do its job. Something went wrong on the spacecraft before it could be put into orbit around the red planet, Mars, and no signals came back.

Failure, Adriana saw, was part of scientific exploration. You learned from the experience, tried again, and never gave up. Persistence was key.

Not all of Adriana's NASA responsibilities related to space. When she made her best-known discovery, she was using images collected by Earth-orbiting satellites. Studying pictures of an area near the town of Chicxulub on Mexico's Yucatan Peninsula, Adriana saw a geological formation that was oddly symmetrical, a very large semicircle. This was 1989, and by then Adriana knew a lot about interpreting pictures taken by satellites. She suspected what she was seeing were cenotes, or sinkholes, formed in limestone.

What would cause the large semicircular pattern? Adriana knew that one explanation was an asteroid impact. And if an asteroid was responsible, Adriana might be seeing direct evidence of the solution to a prehistoric murder mystery: What killed the dinosaurs?

People had known for a long time that something like three-quarters of the Earth's species went extinct at the end of the geologic period known as the Cretaceous, 66 million years ago. In the early 1980s, several scientists speculated that the cause might have been an asteroid striking the Earth.

One piece of evidence for this was the presence on Earth of a mineral called iridium in a layer of clay dating from that time. Iridium is rare near the surface of the Earth but plentiful in asteroids. The iridium in the layer of clay might be asteroid dust—a remnant of the long-ago impact.

Of course, such a crash would also leave a scar, a crater. Where was the crater?

On that day in 1989, Adriana suspected she had found it. In the years since, further study by Adriana and others has shown she was right. Why did the crater stay hidden for so long? In the millions of years since it formed, part was covered by the ocean and part buried in sediment. It took a satellite's-eye view and Adriana's insight to recognize the half ring of cenotes as a clue to its location.

Eventually, the Chicxulub crater would be shown to be about 124 miles (200 kilometers) across. Later computer models would indicate that an asteroid about 8 miles (12 kilometers) wide slammed into the Earth at a speed of about 67,100 mph (30 kilometers per second), shooting steam, dust, and gravel into the air and vaporizing everything for hundreds of miles around.

Soon after that came tidal waves, earthquakes, and volcanic eruptions. All the smoke and sulfur-rich poison gas dimmed the sun for at least a decade. Without enough sunlight, many plants and small creatures died, which meant starvation for the larger creatures that relied on them for food.

A few species adapted and survived, among them the small mammals that eventually gave rise to primates and humans. Without them, we wouldn't be here now to tell the story.

Around the same time the crater struck, massive volcanoes, the Deccan Traps, erupted in what is now India. These eruptions also spewed carbon dioxide into the air and dimmed the sunlight. Whether the eruptions, the asteroid, or a combination of the two caused the extinctions is today disputed by scientists, who continue to research the subject. As is the case with Vera Rubin's dark matter (see page 34), this dispute ultimately will move science forward and contribute to human knowledge.

After the initial discovery of the crater using satellite images, Adriana and other geologists made five expeditions to study the deposits around the Chicxulub crater. Nearby, they found two layers of ejecta—rock melted by the crash that spattered and then flowed outward and formed lobes.

Ejecta lobes are common on Mars, and Adriana was excited to find these on Earth. It was like seeing a bit of Mars in Mexico.

Over time, Adriana and her colleagues have found new evidence of asteroid strikes on Earth. In 2006, radar onboard the space shuttle found another chain of craters in Chad, a country in Africa. These apparently were formed by the impact of a fragmented asteroid or comet in the even more distant past—400 million years ago.

Is it a coincidence that another mass extinction occurred about this time? Adriana believes the Chad impact was too small to be responsible for a widespread catastrophe, but perhaps it was part of a larger event like a comet shower. Either way, it's another example of the close link between the Earth and what's beyond.

In 2018, Adriana was still looking to the sky, managing NASA projects focused on Venus, Jupiter, and Pluto. By learning everything she can about the formation and history of the Earth and the solar system, she expects to get clues about what the future holds for our planet and for the solar system.

ADRIANA OCAMPO

Achievement: Planetary geologist who codiscovered the crater made by a killer asteroid 66 million years ago; program executive for space missions providing insights into the formation of planets and the solar system.

Quote: "It is the dream of every child to play in the dirt. We geologists get to do it for real. We don't explore places; we explore time, way back in the past and on into the future. All that is written in the rocks."

Fascinating fact: Eight-year-old Adriana liked to read to her dog, Tauro. One of their favorite books was Jules Verne's *From the Earth to the Moon*, written in 1865.

SUSAN SOLOMON
CHEMIST AND CLIMATE SCIENTIST
BORN 1956

IT'S JUST A TV show, but it changes one girl's life.

The year is 1966, and the girl is watching a documentary special about the ocean with her parents. It stars a French explorer with a beaky nose, and relies on a combination of story line, nature photography, and science. Over the next decade, the show will become a series that captures a huge audience and introduces millions of viewers to lobsters and sharks, whales and underwater volcanoes, sunken treasure and sea birds.

The girl glued to the screen lives in Chicago. She comes from what she calls an ordinary family—her dad is an insurance salesman, her mom a fourth-grade teacher. But one day she will become an explorer and scientist just like Jacques Cousteau, the French guy on TV. Instead of a watchman's cap, she will wear long underwear, a red windproof suit, and mukluks.

Susan Solomon was ten years old when the first episodes of *The Undersea World of Jacques Cousteau* appeared and inspired her, along with many other young viewers, to become a marine biologist.

While Susan did go on to learn how to scuba dive, she eventually came to a disappointing realization: She was just not that into biology. Susan liked it when the answer to a problem was either this or that. In biology, it seemed more often to be maybe this or maybe that.

Chemistry was better. Chemistry was certain. "You have a clear acidic solution and you add an exact amount of base and wow, it changes to a bright color every time—just like it's supposed to," she later said.

As a senior in high school, Susan learned that she liked research and had a knack for it. In an international science competition, she won a prize for using light to calculate how much oxygen there was in a combination of gases. Studying the atmosphere of Jupiter in college, she became interested in atmospheric science. It was thrilling, she thought, that a person on Earth could learn about the atmospheres of other planets.

Susan earned a doctorate in chemistry and went to work for the National Oceanic and Atmospheric Administration (NOAA) in Colorado. That's where she was in 1985 when British scientists announced the discovery of what later became known as a hole in the ozone layer over Antarctica.

Ozone is oxygen with three atoms per molecule instead of the usual two. It's poisonous if you breathe too much, but in the stratosphere, more than seven miles above the Earth, a layer of it absorbs solar rays that would otherwise damage or even destroy life on the surface.

In the 1970s, two scientists, Mario Molina and Sherwood Rowland, had suggested that man-made chemicals called chlorofluorocarbons (CFCs) might be harming the layer of ozone surrounding the Earth. CFCs were once used in air conditioners, among other things. Molina and Rowland's idea was that sunlight broke apart the CFC molecules, releasing chlorine atoms, which reacted with ozone to make a chlorine oxide. Chlorine oxide then reacted with oxygen to release more chlorine atoms, which reacted with more ozone . . . over and over and over, eating up more and more ozone every time.

In other words, introducing CFCs into the atmosphere had set off a chain reaction that was disastrous for ozone. But if CFCs were the cause, why was ozone disappearing fastest above Antarctica? Few people lived there, and no one used air conditioning!

At her office at NOAA, Susan used a computer to model the situation and came up with what she thought was the reason: High above the South Pole are clouds that contain ice crystals. The crystals' shapes include tiny solid surfaces, which provide platforms for chemical reactions, making these reactions happen much faster than they otherwise would.

To find out if she was right, in August 1986 Susan led a team of sixteen scientists to McMurdo Base in Antarctica. When their Navy pilot learned Susan was in charge, he was so surprised that he was speechless. Susan was thirty years old—young to have such a big responsibility—and she was also the only woman. "Oh!" the pilot said after staring for a minute. "Good for you."

August is winter in the southern hemisphere. McMurdo is close to the South Pole, and the August sun never quite rises. Susan and her colleagues collected samples of the light from the moon and the dim twilight sky above them, then analyzed the samples, working in the dark, often at temperatures as cold as fifty degrees below zero.

In spite of the difficult conditions, Susan and most of her colleagues loved it there. She called the landscape "an incredible, beautiful crystalline palace of white."

It took two expeditions, but at last Susan's team confirmed that CFCs really were the problem. Because of the danger posed by solar radiation, the research soon prompted an international agreement that banned CFCs. Since then, the ozone layer has begun to recover.

In 2002, Susan was again tapped to be in charge. With a Chinese colleague, Qin Dahe, she oversaw preparation of a study by 152 scientists from thirty countries—the United Nations' Intergovernmental Panel on Climate Change.

After six years of nonstop work, the panel released a report concluding that average global temperatures are undoubtedly rising, and human actions are the main cause. The report has been called one of the most influential scientific documents in history.

Climate change is complicated. In brief, the overall temperature on Earth is rising because of increasing amounts of carbon in the atmosphere. Some gases that contain carbon, like methane and carbon dioxide, raise temperatures because they trap the sun's heat very effectively. Carbon dioxide is emitted into the atmosphere when carbon-based fuels like oil and gas are burned.

Climate change has the potential to cause catastrophe, and you might think working on it would be depressing.

Susan doesn't see it that way.

When she became a professor at the Massachusetts Institute of Technology in 2011, she told her students that the fast-changing climate makes this an especially exciting and gratifying time to be a scientist. Susan is an optimist, confident that human ingenuity will prevail.

SUSAN SOLOMON

Achievement: Chemist and climate scientist who substantiated the theory that a man-made chemical was tearing a hole in the atmosphere, leading to a ban of that chemical; also chaired the international panel of scientists that established that human activity is driving climate change.

Quote: "What's great about atmospheric science is that it's a planetary issue. We don't have to be distracted by the politics. There's so much we can agree on."

Fascinating fact: For weeks as she finalized the work of an international panel on climate change, Susan worked long hours with very little sleep. When at last the work was done, Susan made a new goal for herself: Get out in nature and learn to fish.

CAROL GREIDER

MOLECULAR BIOLOGIST
BORN 1961

SHE'S TEN YEARS OLD, and her physics professor father has moved the family to Heidelberg, Germany, for a year. Life in an apartment in the hilly old city is very different from life in their house in flat Davis, California. She doesn't speak any German.

How is she even supposed to find her school?

Her dad's attitude is the same as usual: You'll figure it out.

And so she does.

A little more than a decade later, when she's a graduate student working in a university lab, she'll call on that same self-reliance to help her discover an enzyme, telomerase, that is crucial to the health of cells in organisms from protozoa to people.

Eventually, she will share a Nobel Prize for her discovery.

Carol Greider turned ten in 1971. By then, she had been figuring things out on her own for a while. Her mother, who suffered from depression, died when she was six. Her father loved her and her brother, Mark, and he encouraged them, but he also worked a lot.

At home in California, Carol and Mark walked to school by themselves. In Heidelberg, they learned the bus system, then rode city buses to school, where the classes were taught in German.

By Christmastime, they were getting along fine in their new language, and they had made friends in the big apartment building where they lived. Using string pulleys, they passed notes to kids who lived on the lower floors. Sometimes they banged on the radiators to communicate with them in code—and got in trouble for making so much noise.

From the time she started school in California, Carol had thought of herself as different, even stupid. She had trouble learning to read, write, and especially, spell. Once a week she was called out of class for special tutoring. It was embarrassing.

Much later, Carol found out she had a learning challenge called dyslexia, which makes it hard to relate speech sounds with words and letters. By then, she had come up with a way to cope on her own. She couldn't sound out syllables the way other kids did, so she memorized whole words and how they are spelled—thousands of them. She got really good at memorizing, which turned out to be helpful in science and other classes later on.

In Germany, Carol was different because she was American. Her best German friend, Jiska, was different too. All the other kids at school were Christian, but Jiska was Jewish. When Carol returned to California and started junior high, she realized she herself didn't mind being different. Instead of trying to be one of the cool kids, she picked friends like Jiska, friends who were interesting.

In high school, Carol considered herself a nerd—but not a science nerd, not one of the kids who went home to her chemistry set. Instead, she was president of the American Field Service club, which promoted international understanding.

Most of Carol's friends went to college in Northern California, but Carol—once again—wanted to be different. She left home for Santa Barbara, which is on the Southern California coast, planning to study marine biology. Her first project was about sand crabs, but it involved a lot of counting and observing. She found this boring. She wanted to think creatively, to make things happen, to do experiments.

A professor and friend of the family, Bea Sweeny, suggested she try working in a lab. Bingo—she liked everything about it, including the friendly people who worked with her.

In graduate school, Carol joined a lab run by one of the top cell biologists in the world, Elizabeth Blackburn. Elizabeth and her colleagues were studying chromosomes, the molecules within a cell that contain genetic information.

More specifically, they were looking at telomeres, structures on the ends of chromosomes that seemed to help protect them from damage. When cells divided, each telomere lost bits of its DNA. But something enabled some telomeres to regain their length. What was that something? Could it be an enzyme?

It wasn't clear that the answer to this question would do anybody any practical good. Still, it was interesting and basic to biology, so Carol decided to investigate. Looking back later, she called the quest a dive into the unknown.

Like Elizabeth, Carol studied *Tetrahymena*, single-cell organisms that motor around in fresh water. They make good subjects for telomere research because each contains around 40,000 chromosomes. Carol had to figure out what experiments to do and how to carry them out. She worked twelve-hour days and taught herself DNA cloning and enzyme purification in the process.

But she also found time for fun. She bicycled and competed in triathlons. She went out for lattes with her colleagues. They played practical jokes on each other, wrote skits, and found any excuse for a party.

No one else was working on Christmas Day in 1984 when Carol went into her lab to check an autoradiograph of her latest experiment. An autoradiograph is a special kind of image that shows the chemistry behind a process, in this case the elongation of a telomere. Looking at the image, Carol recognized a pattern indicating the presence of an enzyme. Could it be the one she was looking for?

Carol couldn't be sure. It would take several more months before she and Elizabeth confirmed the presence of an enzyme and came up with a name, telomerase. But that day Carol was excited enough to celebrate. She went home, put on Bruce Springsteen's "Born in the USA," and danced.

In the following years, Carol and others learned that telomeres limit the number of times a cell can divide, making them critically important to understanding aging, cancer, and other diseases. What at first appeared to be only a curiosity-driven science question is in fact fundamental to developing new medical treatments.

For their work on telomeres, Carol, Elizabeth, and Jack Szostak shared the Nobel Prize for medicine or physiology in 2009. By the time she received the huge honor, Carol was a professor at Johns Hopkins University with two children, Gwendolyn and Charles. When the university held a press conference to announce that she had won, she brought her children with her and made sure they appeared in the newspaper photos.

"How many men have won the Nobel in the last few years, and they have kids the same age as mine, and their kids aren't in the picture?" she told an interviewer at the time. "That's a big difference, right? And that makes a statement."

CAROL GREIDER

Achievement: Molecular biologist who discovered an enzyme that protects cells from deterioration, leading to an entirely new field of study with implications for prolonging life and curing disease.

Quote: "When young women ask my advice about, 'Can I be a scientist and have a family and a career?' I tell them, 'Absolutely. You should do what you love to do. And then you have to find the path and the way to go and do that.' And I don't say it's going to be easy."

Fascinating fact: One day in 2009 Carol was up at dawn folding laundry when she got a phone call from Sweden. It was still early when she hung up, but she woke her children. "I won the Nobel Prize," she told them. "You can go back to sleep now."

MAY-BRITT MOSER
NEUROSCIENTIST
BORN 1963

IN SUMMER, THE SUN shines as much as twenty hours in a day on the beautiful and remote Norwegian island of Bergsøy. With school out, most of the girl's friends go away on vacation, but her family doesn't have the money for such luxuries.

She is the youngest of five children. Her father is a carpenter. Her mother minds the farm and the children. They don't even have a car.

The little girl doesn't really mind staying home. She is happy most of the time and curious all the time. When she plays outside, she studies her fellow creatures, even the snails, and wonders what they are thinking about.

As an adult, May-Britt Moser will still be wondering, but by then she'll have her own lab and the tools to get answers. Instead of snails, she will spend a lot of time observing rats. Her insights into how they think will provide important clues to how humans think as well.

May-Britt's mother liked to tell her fairy tales, but when she did, she left out the scary parts. A favorite were the ones about Askeladden, which means "ash boy" in Norwegian. He was smart, kind, and hardworking. He didn't have much money, but he succeeded in life.

May-Britt believed that she could succeed in life too. She also believed in the example of her parents, who worked hard and told her it was working and learning that made them happy.

Thinking she might want to be a doctor, May-Britt went to university in Oslo, the Norwegian capital. There she became friends with Edvard Moser, a boy from another Norwegian island. Soon he became her husband and science collaborator.

May-Britt and Edvard both loved the outdoors and travel. And they both wanted to study the workings of the brain. "We had this crazy energy, this drive to know," she said many years later. "It wasn't just Edvard, or just me, it was the two of us together."

Neither May-Britt or Edvard had much practical experience with brains when they asked an expert on the subject to take them on as students. He hesitated, but they insisted and even hung out in his office until he agreed to give them a chance.

Then, like the gatekeeper in a fairy tale, he gave them an almost impossible task: Build a maze for a rat experiment. An underwater maze. Make it six feet across and eighteen inches tall.

You can't just go to the store and buy parts for a water maze for rats. May-Britt and Edvard had to build it from scratch.

May-Britt said, "This is crazy!"

But they did it.

In the process, they learned a lot—not only about plumbing and carpentry, but eventually about how rats behave underwater, how to clean rat cages, and the best way look at cells in a rat brain.

By the time May-Britt and Edvard earned their doctoral degrees, they were married and had two daughters, Isabel and Ailin. For a while they lived and did research in Scotland. Often, May-Britt sat with a daughter in her lap as she watched the rats playing or navigating mazes.

Some of May-Britt's early research showed that the brains of rats that live with interesting toys and activities are structurally different from the brains of rats with no toys and nothing to do. These busier rats also have superior spatial memories.

The research May-Britt is best known for built on the work of a professor she and Edvard had collaborated with in London, John O'Keefe. In 1971 John and a colleague identified the brain's place cells. Located in a structure called the hippocampus, they enable a rat—or a person—to recognize their surroundings and find their way. ("Hippocampus" means seahorse, which describes the shape of the brain structure.)

In 1997, May-Britt and Edvard decided to take the next logical step and find out how information flowed to the place cells. By this time, they had their own lab in Trondheim, one of the northernmost cities in Norway. They started their project by taking advantage of the fact that cells communicate using tiny electrical charges. That means you can attach electricity sensors to the head of a subject and watch brain cells at work.

That's what May-Britt and her colleagues did with their rats. Then they let the rats loose in a small enclosure. When a brain cell was active, its location in the brain showed up as a dot on a computer screen.

May-Britt is a big fan of chocolate, and by this time she knew that rats are, too. To encourage her rats to move around, she scattered bits of Choco Loops cereal.

It took many, many careful and painstaking experiments over many years to gather good information. At first May-Britt thought the cells she was looking for were in the hippocampus with the place cells, but that turned out to be wrong. Even when the right part of the brain was identified, placing the sensors precisely was hard. But finally she got the answer she sought—and more.

First of all, she learned that the rat's sense of its location was collected in a region of the brain called the entorhinal cortex, and that it flowed from there to the place cells in the hippocampus.

Beyond that, she learned how the cells in the entorhinal cortex operated. It wasn't what the rat saw or smelled or felt that made the cells active, it was how the rat moved. That is, if it turned left and went two steps, the cells did one thing. If it turned around and walked backward, they did another.

When May-Britt and her colleagues gave the rats more room to move around, they learned something amazing. Particular cells fired when the rat crossed a certain point on the ground. When it crossed another point, different cells lit up.

In other words, the rat's brain was creating its own imaginary grid on the floor, then the rat relied on that grid to get around. Over and over as the scientists watched the moving rats, the dots on their computer screens made six-pointed honeycomb patterns that resembled the board for Chinese checkers.

May-Britt and Edvard knew they had made an exciting discovery. For the first time, they had seen a brain translate the real world into its own thought world. This was a giant step toward understanding all the other things brains do.

Since ancient times, people have used a trick related to location to help with memorization. Maybe you know this trick. If you want to remember a long grocery list, for example, think of the different items in different locations in your house—toothpaste on your pillow, chocolate bars on the dining room table, milk in your top dresser drawer. When you're shopping, mentally walk through your house and pick up the items.

May-Britt and Edvard's research suggests that this trick may be effective because memory and location are closely linked in the brain. That link may also explain why people in the early stages of Alzheimer's disease, which affects memory, often get lost.

Later, May-Britt and her colleagues would find more cells with similar jobs, including some that reacted when the rat turned its head and some that reacted when it came near the boundary of its enclosure. They even discovered what you might call the speedometer in the entorhinal cortex: cells that change their activity depending on how fast the rat is moving. All of these worked together with the place cells in the hippocampus to help the rat navigate.

In 2014, May-Britt, Edvard, and John won the Nobel Prize in medicine or physiology for their achievement.

May-Britt Moser married her prince, traveled the world, raised beautiful daughters, and won the biggest prize in science. Her life sounds like the fairy tales her mother read to her as a child.

But real life is not a fairytale. In 2016, she and Edvard divorced.

Even so, they are still parents who love their two daughters—and the four are often together as they continue to study the brain in Trondheim, Norway. There is always more work to do. And in the end, May-Britt agrees with her parents: Work and learning new things make her happy.

MAY-BRITT MOSER

Achievement: Neuroscientist who identified grid cells, the neurons in the brain that track movement, and showed how they enable mammals to find their way—a critical step in understanding human memory and thought.

Quote: "Just to walk (somewhere), we have to understand where we are now, where we want to go, when to turn and when to stop. It's incredible that we are not permanently lost."

Fascinating fact: To attend the Nobel Prize ceremony, May-Britt wore a designer-made satin and leather dress imprinted with sequins. Not only did the sequins form the pattern of firing neurons, they blinked when caught by a camera flash, exactly the way neurons do during calcium imaging in her lab.

MARYAM MIRZAKHANI

MATHEMATICIAN

1977-2017

IT SEEMS AS IF the war has been going on her whole life. She is used to the air raid sirens, the blackouts, the explosions at night, the news that family friends have been killed.

Even though her own family is well-off, the war has created shortages, and there are many things you can't buy in the stores.

Instead of being afraid, the girl with the gray-blue eyes immerses herself in books and watches television biographies of strong women like Marie Curie and Helen Keller.

She also tells herself stories. Most feature a remarkable girl, a world traveler or a brave leader—perhaps the mayor of a great city like Tehran where she lives. Guess who plays the hero? She does! And her hero is always destined to do some great thing.

Maryam Mirzakhani enjoyed making up stories so much that she thought she'd be a writer when she grew up.

But then she discovered math. One teacher told her she wasn't that good at it, but she kept trying—eventually becoming one of the most brilliant, original, and celebrated mathematicians of her time.

Later, she would compare doing math to writing a novel. The problems were like characters you got to know better the longer you worked with them. Looking back, you realized how different they were from what you first expected.

Maryam was three years old when her country, Iran, was invaded by its neighbor, Iraq. War raged for eight years, and at least half a million people were killed. Soldiers weren't the only ones who died. Cities were attacked with missiles and even chemical weapons. Kids as young as thirteen were drafted to fight.

The war ended in 1988, when Maryam was eleven. The timing was lucky, she thought. In middle school, things were comparatively normal for her and her friends. They could concentrate on their studies.

When they were in ninth grade, Maryam and her best friend, Roya Beheshti, heard about Math Olympiad, an international competition for high school students. For fun, the two girls tried some problems from the competition. They solved about half, which they thought was pretty good, considering they had never done anything like it. Excited by the idea of competing, they went to the principal of their all-girls school, who agreed to arrange classes to prepare them for the next one.

In 1994, Maryam was the first girl ever chosen for Iran's Math Olympiad team. The competition was in Singapore, and she earned a gold medal. At the 1995 competition in Toronto, Canada, she earned another one, as well as a perfect score.

Maryam studied math at college in Tehran and came to the United States for graduate work. Her American teachers and colleagues noticed that she asked questions—lots of them—in English but took notes in her native language, Farsi. Over the next twelve years, she became a professor in California, married a computer scientist, and gave birth to a daughter, Anahita.

Maryam did not brag about her abilities or her work. In fact, she called herself slow. According to her colleagues, she was only slow because she took on problems so hard that everybody else had given up. She didn't mind if a problem took years to solve. She was always optimistic that eventually she would succeed. "Life," she said, "is not supposed to be easy."

In graduate school, Maryam became fascinated with a kind of hyperbolic (curved) surface called a Riemann surface—a shape sort of like a crazy multihole pretzel. While these pretzels don't exist in the real world, the rules describing their properties are basic to geometry, and also help in understanding other kinds of math, science, and engineering.

In later work, Maryam studied the way a ball or similar object moves when it's confined in a polygon. Like the crazy pretzels, these are not real balls in real polygons. They are more like the *idea* of a ball in the idea of a polygon. To understand this better, you can picture a billiard ball on a billiard table. The ball rolls in a straight line, hits the side, then ricochets, rolling in another straight line.

Mathematicians have lots of questions about the workings of a system like this. For example, if the ball just kept rolling and ricocheting and rolling and ricocheting forever, would it eventually trace the exact same path again?

Working with professors Alex Eskin and Amir Mohammadi, Maryam wrote a paper that included a theorem solving this problem. This theorem is so useful when it comes to other kinds of problems that some people call it the "magic wand." The paper, published in 2014, is 200 pages long.

To help her visualize the crazy shapes she worked with, Maryam would draw on huge sheets of paper spread out on the floor of her house. Drawing, she said, kept her focused on big issues instead of less important details. When Maryam was at work, her daughter, Anahita, said her mom was painting.

In 2014, Maryam went to South Korea to receive the Fields Medal, the most prestigious award in mathematics. The award has been given at four-year intervals since 1936, and Maryam was the first woman to win it.

At the ceremony, one of her former professors made a speech about how great she was. As he stood at the podium, he noticed Maryam in the audience. She wasn't paying much attention to him. She was busy whispering with her very excited daughter.

Maryam Mirzakhani died of breast cancer in 2017. She was forty years old.

A few months before she died, a friend visited, and the two of them took a walk together. Maryam frequently had to stop, lie down on a bench, and rest. The friend felt terrible for her. At the same time, the friend had been thinking about a math problem and couldn't resist bringing it up. Sick and in pain, Maryam listened and offered ideas and suggestions. Until the very end of her life, Maryam was a generous friend—and she was thinking about math.

MARYAM MIRZAKHANI

Achievement: Mathematician who devised proofs explaining paths on curved surfaces, including changing surfaces, revealing basic truths about geometry and algebra that have ramifications in physics, cosmology, biology, engineering, and other fields.

Quote: "You have to spend some energy and effort to see the beauty of math."

Fascinating fact: Maryam's sixth-grade teacher told her she would never get anywhere studying math because she wasn't that good at it. Maryam was discouraged for a while, but eventually gave math another try. Twenty-five years later, Maryam was the first woman ever to earn the world's highest award for achievement in mathematics, the Fields Medal.

AFTERWORD:
SO YOU WANT TO BE A SCIENTIST

DO YOU WANT TO be an awesome scientist or mathematician like the ones in this book?

Doing research on the people in these pages, I noticed some similarities in how they grew up.

Based on those similarities, I offer the following tips. While I don't absolutely promise they'll get you a Nobel Prize or a Fields Medal, I do promise they will make your life more interesting.

1. Read! It was a book for adults, *The Microbe Hunters*, that convinced young Gertrude Elion she wanted to be a microbiologist. As a girl, Maryam Mirzakhani read every book she could find and thought she would grow up to be a writer. Patricia Bath read the newspaper every day. Sylvia Earle buried herself in the encyclopedia every evening before bed.

2. Work with your hands. Almost every scientist in this book liked to make or build things when she was young. Joan Procter grew up to design zoo habitats but started out designing and building houses for her pets. Jocelyn Bell Burnell, who built a radio telescope when she was a graduate student, liked to build with Meccano sets when she was a girl. Adriana Ocampo liked to work with her dad, an electrician, in his workshop. Ingrid Daubechies made doll clothes.

3. Spend time outdoors looking around. Almost every scientist in this book played outdoors a lot as a girl, and many had collections of eggs, reptiles, insects, or other critters. Ellen Swallow Richards, May-Britt Moser, and Sylvia Earle all grew up on farms.

4. Be brave. Oceanographer Sylvia Earle enjoys swimming with sharks and once kicked an aggressive one in the nose. During World War II, chemist Rosalind Franklin bicycled to work in London even as bombs fell around her. Frankie Kelsey faced down a powerful corporation and won.

5. Make the best of things. Biologist Carol Greider has a learning disability that makes it impossible to sound out words. To learn to spell, she had to memorize long lists of words. Later, when she had to memorize biology terms, it was pretty easy. Tu Youyou had tuberculosis as a teenager and had to take two years off from school. In that time, she learned the value of good health and decided to devote her life to medicine. When others took credit for Rosalind Franklin's most important discovery, she went to work on another project in another lab.

6. Tolerate tedious work. Marie Tharp tallied thousands of depth readings of the ocean floor. Christiane Volhard looked at endless numbers of fruit fly embryos. Jocelyn Bell Burnell read miles of printouts from her radio telescope. Ellen Richards tested 40,000 water samples. All of them stayed focused and put up with tedium by keeping in mind their larger goals—mapping the ocean floor, understanding how genes work, exploring outer space, drinking clean water.

7. Think for yourself. Lynn Margulis, Vera Rubin, Marie Tharp, and Frankie Kelsey were ridiculed for their ideas, but they refused to back down and were vindicated. During World War II, Rosalind Franklin's father told her to quit her science job and volunteer on a farm. He said that was the patriotic thing to do. Rosalind thought she could do more good for the war effort studying coal than picking vegetables, and she was right.

8. Don't give up on science if it turns out you're not good at something. Frankie Oldham Kelsey couldn't get the hang of high school chemistry. May-Britt Moser's grades weren't good enough for medical school. Christiane Volhard thought college physics was too hard. Instead of giving up, each stepped back, took a look at her strengths, and tried something new.

9. Be ready to power past obstacles. In fact, if possible, ignore them. Looking back at her career, Susan Solomon said she probably was discriminated against as a woman, but she was too focused on her work to notice. Ellen Richards suffered crippling depression in her twenties, but rallied and went to college. Excluded from a study group as a first-year student at college, Shirley Ann Jackson later started a program to help students who needed help.

10. Use your imagination. As a child, Adriana Ocampo built a spaceship using a sheet and a space colony using pots and pans. Both Vera Rubin and Maryam Mirzakhani drew giant pictures to help them understand the problems they were working on.

11. Find a mentor who supports you. Almost all the scientists in this book gave credit to teachers, professors, or other colleagues for inspiring and helping them. May-Britt Moser, whose maiden name is Andreassen, still remembers a high school teacher who would call on her and say, "Miss Andreassen, you know the answer. I believe in you!"

12. Because you know there will be failures, celebrate your successes. As Rosalind Franklin put it, "What's the point of doing all this work if you don't get some fun out of it?"

13. Finally, be curious about science and everything else. As children, all the scientists in these pages were fascinated by the natural world and asked a ton of questions. When they grew up and pursued their careers, their curiosity only increased. As Sylvia Earle tweeted in 2017, "Scientists never stop asking. They're little kids who never grew up."

GLOSSARY

AMINO ACID: A chemical compound found in living cells that contains carbon, oxygen, hydrogen, and nitrogen. Sometimes amino acids link to form proteins.

ANABOLIC: In living things, bringing simple molecules together to make increasingly complex ones.

ARTEMISININ: An extract from the sweet wormwood plant that is an effective treatment for malaria.

ASTEROID: A space rock orbiting the sun that's smaller than a planet but bigger than a meteorite.

ATMOSPHERE: The gases surrounding a planet, such as Earth.

ATOM: The smallest unit of an element, which may bind with other atoms to form molecules. Atoms are made of even smaller particles: protons and electrons. All but hydrogen, the simplest, also have neutrons.

BACTERIA: Single-cell life forms that lack a nucleus. Found everywhere, they are the most abundant form of life on Earth.

BIOLOGY: The study of living things.

CATABOLIC: In living things, breaking down complex molecules into more simple ones.

CATARACT: A cloudy covering over the lens of the eye.

CELL: The basic unit of a living thing. A cell always has a membrane to hold it together. Some organisms, like people and petunias, are made up of many cells that do different jobs. Others, like bacteria and amoebae, are made up of only one cell.

CENOTE: A hole in the ground formed when the bedrock collapses, also called a sinkhole.

CHARGE: A particle's tendency either to attract or repel. In an atom, electrons carry a negative charge while protons carry a positive charge. A proton and an electron are drawn to each other, while two protons or two electrons repel each other.

CHEMICAL: A substance with its own distinctive molecular composition.

CHEMISTRY: The study of the elements—what they're made of, how they're structured, and what they do when they get together.

CHLOROFLUOROCARBONS (CFCS): Gases once used in refrigerators, air conditioners, and aerosol sprays. Sunlight causes them to decompose in the atmosphere, damaging the layer of ozone that protects life on Earth from excessive sunlight.

CHLOROPLASTS: The tiny structures (organelles) inside plant cells that perform photosynthesis—use energy from sunlight to convert carbon dioxide and water into sugar, releasing oxygen in the process.

CHROMOSOMES: Strands of DNA that contain genes.

COMET: An icy object that orbits the sun and sometimes has a tail made of water vapor.

CORNEA: The transparent front part of the eye that covers the iris and the pupil.

CRYSTAL: A solid material made up of atoms arranged in a three-dimensional repeating pattern.

CRYSTALLOGRAPHY: A photographic method that uses X-rays instead of light to make a picture; it can be used to reveal the molecular structure of a material.

CULTURAL REVOLUTION: From 1966 to 1976, the Chinese government's radical attempt to eliminate certain ideas and remake citizens into good members of a new kind of society. Many people had to leave home or suffered in other ways.

DARK MATTER: Unseen matter theorized to make up the vast majority of the universe, detectable because of its effects on light and the force of gravity.

DIAMETER: A straight line from one side of a circle to the other, crossing through the center.

DNA (DEOXYRIBONUCLEIC ACID): The molecule in a cell that carries instructions to tell proteins in the cell what to do. The information in DNA is stored as a code made up of four chemical bases: adenine (A), guanine (G), cytosine (C), and thymine (T). The structure of DNA is a double helix, two ladder-like strands twisted into a spiral. The rungs of the ladder are pairs of the chemical bases, either adenine and thymine, or guanine and cytosine.

DYSLEXIA: A learning disorder that makes it hard to relate speech sounds with words and letters.

ELECTRON: A subatomic particle with a negative charge. Electrons orbit the nuclei of atoms and may jump from one to another, in which case, voilà! Electric current.

ELEMENT: A material that can't be broken into simpler components by chemical means. All of the atoms in an element have the same number of protons (positively charged particles). Oxygen, gold, potassium, and uranium are examples of elements.

EMBRYO: A creature before it is hatched or born.

ENZYME: A cell protein that acts on other molecules to affect metabolism.

EUKARYOTE: A cell with a nucleus. Animal and plant cells are eukaryotes, for example. Bacteria are not.

EXTINCTION: The total disappearance of a species or organism.

FIELDS MEDAL: Named for Canadian mathematician John Charles Fields, the Fields Medal is one of the most prestigious awards in mathematics. It's given at four-year intervals by the International Mathematical Union to two, three, or four mathematicians under the age of forty.

FOSSIL: What's left of a thing that lived long ago. It might be preserved bone or tissue, or an imprint in a rock.

FOSSIL FUELS: Fuels like oil, coal, and gas that come from long-buried organic matter that is made mostly of carbon. When those fuels are burned, the carbon is released into the atmosphere.

FREQUENCY: In physics, the rate at which something, like the peak of a wave, occurs. In math, it's the relationship between the number of times something occurs and the possible number of times it could occur.

GENE: The basic unit of heredity, which is transmission of information from an organism to its offspring. Genes are made up of DNA. Humans have between 20,000 and 25,000 genes.

GEODESIC: The shortest distance between two points on a curve.

GRAVITY: The force that causes objects with mass to attract one another.

HIPPOCAMPUS: A structure in the brain that helps with processing emotions and remembering. It is shaped a little like a seahorse.

HORMONES: Chemicals that transmit signals from glands such as the pituitary to locations elsewhere in the body, to stimulate specific cells or tissues into action.

IRAN-IRAQ WAR: Eight-year conflict (1980–1988) between neighboring Middle Eastern countries that caused billions of dollars in damage and killed more than 500,000 people. Neither side won.

LARVA: An insect at a very early stage of development that looks much different from the adult.

LASER: A device that creates an intense beam of a single color of light. Laser beams can be tightly focused and also can travel long distances. (LASER stands for light amplified stimulated emission radiation.)

MECCANO SETS: Toy building sets invented in Britain in 1898, similar to Erector sets, invented in the United States in 1913. Today the two have merged and Meccano is the worldwide brand.

MALARIA: A sometimes fatal blood disease transmitted by female mosquitoes that causes chills and fever.

MAMMAL: Any warm-blooded animal that is born live (not in an egg) and drinks mother's milk when young.

MAO ZEDONG (1893–1976): Leader of the Chinese revolution and eventually the Chinese government.

MASS: The amount of matter in something, sometimes measured in pounds or kilograms.

MATTER: Something solid, liquid, or gaseous that takes up space.

METABOLISM: The chemical processes of life, including breathing, eating, and reproducing.

MITOCHONDRIA: Organelles (small structures) within animal cells that break down food to release energy. Like chloroplasts in plants, mitochondria have their own DNA—separate from the DNA of the organism as a whole—indicating that their ancestors were independent bacteria.

MOLECULE: Two or more atoms that are linked by bonded electrons.

MUTANT: An organism with a mutation.

MUTATION: A random change in a gene that affects how it works.

NEURON: A specialized cell that transmits information in the nervous system or brain of an animal or human.

NEUTRON STAR: A small (roughly six miles in diameter), very dense star that formed at the core of a supernova.

NOBEL PRIZE: Among the most prestigious awards in the world, the three science prizes are given annually for contributions in physiology or medicine, chemistry, and physics. There are also awards for contributions to peace, to literature, and to economics. The awards were established by Swedish inventor and entrepreneur Alfred Nobel in 1895.

OPHTHALMOLOGY: The study of eyes, eyesight, and related diseases.

ORGANELLE: A small structure inside a cell, such as mitochondria and chloroplasts.

ORGANISM: Something that can eat, grow, and reproduce—a living thing.

OZONE: A kind of oxygen with three atoms in its

molecule that's formed in sunlight. High above the Earth, a layer of it protects life from the sun's rays. Nearer the surface, it is a pollutant that is harmful to breathe.

PARASITE: An organism that relies on another organism to live, damaging the other in the process.

PARTICLE: A tiny unit of matter, such as a proton, electron, or quark.

PETRI DISH: A shallow, clear dish used to grow tiny organisms such as bacteria in a lab.

PHOTOSYNTHESIS: The process by which plants and some bacteria transform carbon dioxide and water into sugar, using sunlight. Because plants could not live without photosynthesis and animals could not live without plants, life on Earth depends on photosynthesis.

PHYSICS: The study of matter, energy, space, and time, and how they relate to one another.

PHYSIOLOGY: The study of the anatomy and functions that define a living organism, such as growth, metabolism, and reproduction.

PHYTOCHEMICALS: Chemicals that come from plants.

PITUITARY GLAND: An organ located at the base of the brain that releases hormones that affect growth, birth, emotions, and the release of other hormones.

PROKARYOTE: A simple kind of cell that lacks a nucleus. Bacteria are prokaryotes.

PROTEIN: A complex chemical made of amino acids. Cells are mostly made of proteins, and proteins perform most of the chemical processes required for life.

PULSAR: A rapidly spinning neutron star that emits signals that are read as pulses by radio telescopes.

PURINE: An organic chemical made of carbon and nitrogen. Purines form the basis of many biologically important substances, including two components of DNA, guanine and adenine.

RADIATION: Energy that is emitted in the form of waves or particles, such as photons and electrons, that may result from heat or nuclear reactions.

RADIO TELESCOPE: A scientific instrument that observes the universe by detecting radio waves emitted by objects in space.

RNA (RIBONUCLEIC ACID): An acid used to make proteins in all living cells; RNA carries genetic information in viruses and bacteria.

SPECIES: A group of similar living things with many common traits, that is capable of breeding together.

SPECTROMETER: A device that measures the frequency of radiation.

STRATOSPHERE: The layer of atmosphere that extends from the tropopause, four to twelve miles above the Earth, to about thirty miles above the Earth.

SUPERNOVA: A brightly burning star formed when a supergiant star collapses.

SYNTHESIZE: Bring two or more things together to make a new thing.

TELOMERES: Tails at the ends of chromosomes that are made of DNA. Long telomeres protect a cell's genetic information and may slow aging.

TELOMERASE: A naturally occurring enzyme that lengthens and protects telomeres.

THEORY: A statement that brings together observation and other evidence to explain something that happens or has happened. The statement must be logical and testable. Gravitational theory, evolutionary theory, and plate tectonics theory are examples.

SOURCES

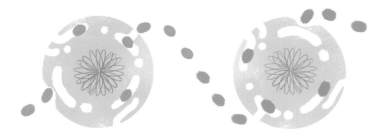

Besides the sources listed below, I am grateful for the input from Dr. Sylvia Earle, Dame Jocelyn Bell Burnell, Dr. Ingrid Daubechies, Dr. May-Britt Moser, Dr. Christiane Volhard, Dr. Patricia Bath, Dr. Adriana Ocampo, Dr. Susan Solomon, and Dr. Carol Greider. It was a thrill for me to correspond with these rock-star scientists.

ELLEN SWALLOW RICHARDS

AMERICAN CHEMISTRY SOCIETY. "Ellen H. Swallow Richards (1842–1911)."
    https://www.acs.org/content/acs/en/education/whatischemistry/women-scientists/ellen-h-swallow
    -richards.html.
HUNT, Caroline L. *The Life of Ellen H. Richards.* Boston: Whitcomb & Barrows, 1912.
NEW YORK TIMES. "Mrs. Ellen H. Richards Dead." March 31, 1911.
    https://timesmachine.nytimes.com/timesmachine/1911/03/31/105024677.pdf.

JOAN BEAUCHAMP PROCTER

ALCHETRON. "Joan Beauchamp Procter." June 28, 2018. https://alchetron.com/Joan-Beauchamp-Procter.
BAILES, Howard. "Procter, Joan Beauchamp." *Oxford Dictionary of National Biography,* 2019.
    https://doi.org/10.1093/ref:odnb/73713.
BOULENGER, E. G. "Obituary: Dr. Joan B. Procter." *Nature,* October 17, 1931.
    https://www.nature.com/nature/journal/v128/n3233/pdf/128664b0.pdf.
MURPHY, James B., and Trooper Walsh. "Dragons and Humans." *Herpetology Review,* 2006, 37(3), 269-275.
SPECTATOR ARCHIVE. "Miss Joan Procter." September 26, 1931. http://archive.spectator.co.uk
    /article/26th-september-1931/3/miss-joan-proctor-we-regret-to-record-the-death-on.
VALDEZ, Patricia. *Joan Procter, Dragon Doctor: The Woman Who Loved Reptiles.* New York: Knopf, 2018.

FRANCES OLDHAM KELSEY

BREN, Linda. "Frances Oldham Kelsey: FDA Medical Reviewer Leaves Her Mark on History." *FDA Consumer,*
    March-April 2001. https://web.archive.org/web/20061020043712
    /http://www.fda.gov/fdac/features/2001/201_kelsey.html.
KELSEY, Frances O., PhD, MD. "Autobiographical Reflections." U.S. Food and Drug Administration.
    https://www.fda.gov/media/89162/download.

SOURCES

MCFADDEN, Robert D. "Frances Oldham Kelsey, Who Saved U.S. Babies from Thalidomide, Dies at 101." *New York Times*, August 7, 2015. https://www.nytimes.com/2015/08/08/science/frances-oldham -kelsey-fda-doctor-who-exposed-danger-of-thalidomide-dies-at-101.html?mcubz=3&_r=2.

NEW YORK TIMES. "Dr. Kelsey Will Receive a High Presidential Award." August 5, 1962. https://timesmachine.nytimes.com/timesmachine/1962/08/05/83500774.html?pageNumber=1.

PERITZ, Ingrid. "Canadian Doctor Averted Disaster by Keeping Thalidomide out of the U.S." *The Globe and Mail*, November 24, 2014. https://beta.theglobeandmail.com/news/national/canadian-doctor-averted -disaster-by-keeping-thalidomide-out-of-the-us/article21721337/?ref=http://www.theglobeandmail.com&.

U.S. FOOD AND DRUG ADMINISTRATION. "Frances Oldham Kelsey: Medical Reviewer Famous for Averting a Public Health Tragedy." February 1, 2018. https://www.fda.gov/AboutFDA/History/VirtualHistory/HistoryExhibits/ucm345094.htm.

GERTRUDE BELLE ELION

ALTMAN, Lawrence K. "Gertrude Elion, Drug Developer, Dies at 81." *New York Times*, February 23, 1999. http://www.nytimes.com/1999/02/23/us/gertrude-elion-drug-developer-dies-at-81.html.

AVERY, Mary Ellen. "Gertrude Belle Elion. 23 January 1918–21 February 1999." *Biographical Memoirs of Fellows of the Royal Society*, The Royal Society Publishing, December 12, 2008. https://doi.org/10.1098/rsbm.2007.0051.

BOUTON, Katherine. "The Nobel Pair." *New York Times Magazine*, January 29, 1989. https://www.nytimes.com/1989/01/29/magazine/the-nobel-pair.html.

LARSEN, Kristine. "Gertrude Elion." *Jewish Women: A Comprehensive Historical Encyclopedia*. March 1, 2009. Jewish Women's Archive. https://jwa.org/encyclopedia/article/elion-gertrude-belle.

NOBEL PRIZE. "Gertrude B. Elion Biographical." Nobelprize.org, 1989. https://www.nobelprize.org/prizes/medicine/1988/elion/biographical/.

ROSALIND FRANKLIN

MADDOX, Brenda. "Nova: Before Watson and Crick." PBS, April 22, 2003. https://www.pbs.org/wgbh/nova/article/before-watson-crick/.

———. *Rosalind Franklin: The Dark Lady of DNA*. New York: HarperCollins, 2002.

NOBEL PRIZE. "The Discovery of the Molecular Structure of DNA—The Double Helix." Nobelprize.org, September 30, 2003. https://www.nobelprize.org/educational/medicine/dna_double_helix/readmore.html.

PBS. "People and Discoveries: Rosalind Franklin." WGBH, 1998. http://www.pbs.org/wgbh/aso/databank /entries/bofran.html.

MARIE THARP

BELL, Danna. "Primary Sources in Science Classrooms: Mapping the Ocean Floor, Marie Tharp, and Making Arguments from Evidence (Part 1)." *Teaching with the Library of Congress*, October 8, 2015, Library of Congress. http://blogs.loc.gov/teachers/2015/10/primary-sources-in-science-classrooms -mapping-the-ocean-floor-marie-tharp-and-making-arguments-from-evidence-part-1/.

BIZZARRO, Danielle. "Lamont-Doherty Earth Observatory Bestows Heritage Award on Marie Tharp, Pioneer of Modern Oceanography." *Columbia News*, July 10, 2001. http://www.columbia.edu/cu/news/01/07/marieTharp.html.

SOURCES

BURLEIGH, Robert. *Solving the Puzzle Under the Sea: Marie Tharp Maps the Ocean Floor.* New York: Simon & Schuster, 2016.

COLUMBIA 250. "C250 Celebrates Columbians Ahead of Their Time: Marie Tharp." 2004. http://c250.columbia.edu/c250_celebrates/remarkable_columbians/marie_tharp.html.

DOEL, Ronald, Tonya Levin, and Mason Marker. "Extending Modern Cartography to the Ocean Depths: Military Patronage, Cold War Priorities, and the Heezen-Tharp Mapping Project, 1952–1959." *Journal of Historical Geography*, 2006, 32(3), 605-626.

FOX, Margalit. "Marie Tharp, Oceanographic Cartographer, Dies at 86." *New York Times*, August 26, 2006. http://www.nytimes.com/2006/08/26/obituaries/26tharp.html.

WOODS HOLE OCEANOGRAPHIC INSTITUTION. "Mary Sears Woman Pioneer in Oceanography Award: Marie Tharp Bio." December 12, 2006. http://www.whoi.edu/sbl/liteSite.do?litesiteid=9092&articleId=13407.

VERA COOPER RUBIN

BARTUSIAK, Marcia. "The Woman Who Spins the Stars." *Discover*, October 1990. http://www.marciabartusiak.com/uploads/8/5/8/9/8589314/spins_the_stars.pdf.

LIGHTMAN, Alan. "Oral Histories: Vera Rubin." American Institute of Physics, April 3, 1989. https://www. aip.org/history-programs/niels-bohr-library/oral-histories/33963.

OVERBYE, Dennis. "Vera Rubin, 88, Dies; Opened Doors in Astronomy, and for Women." *New York Times*, December 27, 2016. https://www.nytimes.com/2016/12/27/science/vera-rubin-astronomist-who -made-the-case-for-dark-matter-dies-at-88.html?_r=0.

———. *Lonely Hearts of the Cosmos: The Story of the Scientific Quest for the Secret of the Universe.* Columbus, Ga.: Back Bay Books, 1999.

SCOLES, Sarah. "How Vera Rubin Confirmed Dark Matter." *Astronomy*, October 4, 2016. http://www. astronomy.com/news/2016/10/vera-rubin.

TU YOUYOU

ANG, Francis Eduard. "Tu Youyou's Childhood Home Now Historical Site." *Yibada*, December 12, 2015. http://en.yibada.com/articles/93993/20151212/tu-youyous-childhood-home-now-historical-site.htm.

DAMBECK, Susanne. "The Modest Nobel Laureate: Tu Youyou." Lindau Nobel Laureate Meetings, October 12, 2015. http://www.lindau-nobel.org/the-modest-nobel-laureate-youyou-tu/.

GUO, Jeff. "How a Secret Chinese Military Drug Based on an Ancient Herb Won the Nobel Prize." *Washington Post*, October 6, 2015. https://www.washingtonpost.com/news/wonk/wp/2015/10/06/how-a -secret-chinese-military-drug-based-on-an-ancient-herb-won-the-nobel-prize/?utm_term=.6d38a2d898e9.

MCKENNA, Phil. "Nobel Prize Goes to Modest Woman Who Beat Malaria for China." *New Scientist*, November 9, 2011. https://www.newscientist.com/article/mg21228382.000-the-modest-woman-who-beat-malaria-for-china/.

MILLER, Louis, and Su Xinzhuan. "Artemisinin: Discovery from the Chinese Herbal Garden." *Cell*, September 16, 2011. https://doi.org/10.1016/j.cell.2011.08.024.

NOBEL PRIZE. "Youyou Tu Biographical." NobelPrize.org, 2015. https://www.nobelprize.org/nobel_prizes/medicine/laureates/2015/tu-bio.html.

PHILLIPS, Tom. "Tu Youyou: How Mao's Challenge to Malaria Pioneer Led to Nobel Prize." *The Guardian*, October 5, 2015. https://www.theguardian.com/science/2015/oct/05 /youyou-tu-how-maos-challenge-to-malaria-pioneer-led-to-nobel-prize.

SOURCES

ZOU, Luxiao. "Chinese Scientist Wins Nobel Prize in Medicine; China Hails the Laureate with Reflection."
People's Daily, October 6, 2015. http://en.people.cn/n/2015/1006/c90000-8958353.html.

TU, Youyou. "The Discovery of Artemisinin (Qinghaosu) and Gifts from Chinese Medicine."
Nature Medicine, 2011, 17(10), xix-xxii.

SYLVIA EARLE

DREISBACH, Shaun. "The Explorer: Sylvia Earle." *Glamour*, November 4, 2014.
https://www.glamour.com/story/sylvia-earle.

EARLE, Sylvia. *The World Is Blue: How Our Fate and the Ocean's Are One*. Washington, D.C.:
National Geographic, 2010.

NATIONAL GEOGRAPHIC EDUCATION. "Oceanographer Sylvia Earle." National Geographic Society,
September 9, 2011. https://www.nationalgeographic.org/news/real-world-geography-sylvia-earle/.

NATIONAL WOMEN'S HALL OF FAME. "Sylvia A. Earle." 2000. https://www.womenofthehall.org
/inductee/sylvia-a-earle/.

NIVOLA, Claire. *Life in the Ocean: The Story of Oceanographer Sylvia Earle*. New York: Farrar, Straus
and Giroux, 2012.

RAFFERTY, John P. "Sylvia Earle, American Oceanographer and Explorer." *Encyclopedia Britannica*, August
26, 2018. https://www.britannica.com/biography/Sylvia-Earle.

ROSENBLATT, Roger. "Sylvia Earle: Call of the Sea." *Time*, October 5, 1998.
http://content.time.com/time/magazine/article/0,9171,989255,00.html.

WHITE, Wallace. "Her Deepness." *The New Yorker*, July 3, 1989. http://archives.newyorker.com
/?i=1989-07-03#folio=044.

LYNN ALEXANDER MARGULIS

BROCKMAN, John. "Lynn Margulis 1938–2011 'Gaia Is a Tough Bitch.'" *Edge*, November 23, 2011.
https://www.edge.org/conversation/lynn_margulis-lynn-margulis-1938-2011-gaia-is-a-tough-bitch.

MARGULIS, Lynn. "Did Sex Emerge from Cannibalism? Sex, Death and Kefir." *Scientific American*,
November 23, 2011. https://www.scientificamerican.com/article/sex-death-kefir-lynn-margulis/.

———. *Symbiotic Planet: A New Look at Evolution*. New York: Basic Books, 1999.

ROSE, Steven. "Lynn Margulis obituary." *The Guardian*, December 11, 2011.
https://www.theguardian.com/science/2011/dec/11/lynn-margulis-obtiuary.

SAGAN, Dorion. *Lynn Margulis: The Life and Legacy of a Scientific Rebel*. Hartford, Vermont: Chelsea
Green Publishing, 2012.

TERESI, Dick. "Discover Interview: Lynn Margulis Says She's Not Controversial, She's Right." *Discover*, June 17,
2011. http://discovermagazine.com/2011/apr/16-interview-lynn-margulis-not-controversial-right.

UNDERSTANDING EVOLUTION. "Endosymbiosis: Lynn Margulis." University of California Museum of
Paleontology and the National Center for Science Education. https://evolution.berkeley.edu/evolibrary
/article/history_24.

WEBER, Bruce. "Lynn Margulis: Trailblazing Theorist on Evolution Dies at 73." *New York Times*,
November 25, 2011. http://www.nytimes.com/2011/11/25/science/lynn-margulis-trailblazing-theorist
-on-evolution-dies-at-73.html.

SOURCES

PATRICIA ERA BATH

BIOGRAPHY.COM Editors. "Patricia Bath Biography." A&E Television Network, February 9, 2018.
   https:// www.biography.com/people/patricia-bath-21038525.

DAVIDSON, Martha. "Innovative Lives: The Right to Sight: Patricia Bath." Smithsonian National Museum
   of American History, March 3, 2005. http://invention.si.edu/innovative-lives-right-sight-patricia-bath.

FAMOUS BLACK INVENTORS. "Dr. Patricia Bath: Fight for the Right to Sight." 2008.
   http://www.black-inventor.com/Dr-Patricia-Bath.asp.

LAMBERT, Laura. "Patricia Bath." In *Inventors and Inventions*, Vol. 1. Tarrytown, New York: Marshall Cavendish, 2008.

LEMELSON-MIT PROGRAM. "Patricia Bath." Resources, Historical Inventors.
   http://lemelson.mit.edu/resources/patricia-bath.

OSMUNDSEN, John A. "28 Science-Minded Teen-Agers Report on Summer of Research." *New York Times*,
   August 31, 1959. https://timesmachine.nytimes.com/timesmachine/1959/08/31/88814439
   .html?ac-tion=click&contentCollection=Archives&module=ArticleEndCTA&region=ArchiveBody&pg
   -type=arti-cle&pageNumber=23.

U.S. NATIONAL LIBRARY OF MEDICINE. "Dr. Patricia E. Bath." *Changing the Face of Medicine*, USA
   . gov, October 14, 2003. https://cfmedicine.nlm.nih.gov/physicians/biography_26.html.

CHRISTIANE NUSSLEIN-VOLHARD

ANGIER, Natalie. "Scientist at Work: Christiane Nusslein-Volhard, 'The Lady of the Flies,' Dives Into a New
   Pond." *New York Times*, December 5, 1995. https://www.nytimes.com/1995/12/05/science
   /scientist-work-christiane-nusslein-volhard-lady-flies-dives-into-new-pond.html.

COLD SPRING HARBOR LABORATORY, DNA Learning Center. "Master Genes Control Basic Body Plans:
   Christiane Nüsslein-Volhard." DNA from the Beginning, 2011. http://www.dnaftb.org/37/bio-2.html.

DREIFUS, Claudia. "Solving a Mystery of Life, Then Tackling a Real-Life Problem." *New York Times*, July 4,
   2006. http://www.nytimes.com/2006/07/04/science/04conv.html.

EDITORS, TheFamousPeople.com. "Christiane Nüsslein-Volhard Biography." TheFamousPeople.com,
   November 9, 2017. https://www.thefamouspeople.com/profiles/christiane-nsslein-volhard-6501.php.

NOBEL PRIZE. "Christiane Nüsslein-Volhard Banquet Speech." Nobelprize.org. 1995. http://www.nobel
   -prize.org/nobel_prizes/medicine/laureates/1995/nusslein-volhard-speech.html.

———. "Christiane Nüsslein-Volhard: Interview Transcript." Nobelprize.org. 1995. http://www.nobelprize
   .org/nobel_prizes/medicine/laureates/1995/nusslein-volhard-interview-transcript.html.

———. "Christiane Nüsslein-Volhard Biographical." Nobelprize.org. 1995. http://www.nobel-prize.org/nobel
   _prizes/medicine/laureates/1995/nusslein-volhard-bio.html.

JOCELYN BELL BURNELL

BBC. Jocelyn Bell Burnell (audio and video clips). http://www.bbc.co.uk/science/space/universe
   /scientists/jocelyn_bell_burnell.

ALLAN, Vicky. "Face to Face: Science Star Who Went Under the Radar of Nobel Prize Judges."
   The Herald, January 4, 2015. http://www.heraldscotland.com/news/13195814.
   Face_to_Face__science_star_who_went_under_the_radar_of_Nobel_Prize_judges/.

BIOGRAPHY.COM Editors. "Jocelyn Bell Burnell Biography." A&E Television Network, February 27, 2018.
   https://www.biography.com/people/jocelyn-bell-burnell-9206018.

SOURCES

DEVORKIN, David. "Jocelyn Bell Burnell." American Institute of Physics, May 21, 2000. https://www.aip.org/history-programs/niels-bohr-library/oral-histories/31792.

STARCHILD TEAM. "Jocelyn Bell Burnell." High Energy Astrophysics Science Archive Research Center at NASA/GSFC, 1999. https://starchild.gsfc.nasa.gov/docs/StarChild/whos_who_level2/bell.html.

WADE, Nicholas. "Was She or Wasn't She?" *The Scientist*, April 2003 https://www.the-scientist.com/closing-bell/was-she-or-wasnt-she-51842.

WEATHERALL, Kate Marsh. "The Woman Who Discovered Pulsars: An Interview with Jocelyn Bell-Burnell." Weatherall Technical Applications, October 26, 1995. http://weatheralltech.com/bell/index.html.

SHIRLEY ANN JACKSON

THE HISTORYMAKERS. "Shirley Ann Jackson." Sciencemakers Video Archive, 2006. http://www.idvl.org/sciencemakers/bio10.html.

NEW YORK TIMES EDUCATION. "Biography of Shirley Ann Jackson, PhD." 2004. https://archive.is/20170301093632/http://www.nytimes.com/ref/college/faculty/coll_pres_jacksonbio.html.

O'CONNELL, Diane. *Strong Force: The Story of Physicist Shirley Ann Jackson*. Washington, D.C.: Joseph Henry Press, 2006.

WASHINGTON POST LIVE. "Jackson Recalls Career Path—from Collecting Bumble Bees to MIT." *Washington Post*, December 6, 2012. https://www.washingtonpost.com/video/postlive/jackson-recalls-career -path---from-collecting-bumble-bees-to-mit/2012/12/06/783e2d98-3fc4-11e2-ae43-cf491b837f7b _video.html?utm_term=.8a886870644b.

INGRID DAUBECHIES

DAUBECHIES, Ingrid. "Using Mathematics to Repair a Masterpiece." *Quanta Magazine*, September 29, 2016. https://www.quantamagazine.org/using-mathematics-to-repair-a-masterpiece-20160929.

DUKE UNIVERSITY. "Ingrid Daubechies." Faculty, 2019. https://ece.duke.edu/faculty/ingrid-daubechies.

FAN, Ken. "Ingrid Daubechies, Part 3." *Girls' Angle Bulletin*, 2008, 2(2). http://www.girlsangle.org/page/ bulletin-archive/GABv02n02E.pdf.

THE FRANKLIN INSTITUTE. "Ingrid Daubechies." The Franklin Institute Awards, April 2011. https://www .fi.edu/laureates/ingrid-daubechies.

HAUNSPERGER, Deanna, and Stephen Kennedy. "Coal Miner's Daughter." *Math Horizons*, April 2000. https://www.maa.org/sites/default/files/pdf/horizons/Coal%20Miners%20Daughter.pdf.

STANCILL, Jane. "Duke Math Professor Wins $1.5 Million Award." *The News & Observer*, August 1, 2016. http://www.newsobserver.com/news/local/education/article93169462.html.

STARCK, Senne. "Flemish Professor on How Maths Can Change the World." *Flanders Today*, October 15, 2014. http://www.flanderstoday.eu/innovation/flemish-professor-how-maths-can-change-world.

WORLD ACADEMY OF SCIENCES. "Maths Is (also) for Women." Internet Archive Wayback Machine, July 29, 2014. https://web.archive.org/web/20151101053356/http://twas.org/article/maths-also-women.

SOURCES

ADRIANA OCAMPO

ALIC, Margaret. "Adriana Ocampo, Planetary Geologist." Contemporary Hispanic Biography, 2003. http://www.encyclopedia.com/education/news-wires-white-papers-and-books /ocampo-adriana-c-1955-planetary-geologist.

COLOMBIA NEW YORK. "Adriana Ocampo, la barranquillera de la NASA al frente de las exploraciones del planeta Plutón." New York, January 20, 2016. http://colombianewyork.com /adriana-ocampo-la-barranquillera-de-la-nasa-al-frente-de-las-exploraciones-del-planeta-pluton/.

DISBROW, Sarah. "Space Geologist Adriana Ocampo." Wonderwise Women in Science Learning Series. http://wonderwise.unl.edu/18space/spacescie.htm.

GRESHKO, Michael. "What Actually Killed the Dinosaurs? Volcanic Clues Heat up Debate." *National Geographic*, Feb. 21, 2019 https://www.nationalgeographic.com/science/2019/02 /what-actually-killed-dinosaurs-volcanoes-heat-up-debate/.

HOPPING, Lorraine Jean. *Space Rocks: The Story of Planetary Geologist Adriana Ocampo*. Women's Adventures in Science, Joseph Henry Press. Washington, D.C., 2006.

MONTEIRO, L. "NASA Scientist Encourages Women to Reach for the Stars." *Waterloo Region Record*, March 8, 2013. https://www.therecord.com/news-story/2625067-nasa-scientist-encourages-women -to-reach-for-the-stars/.

NASA SCIENCE. "Adriana Ocampo, Program Manager, NASA Science Headquarters." March 1, 2015. https://solarsystem.nasa.gov/people/ocampoa.

NATIONAL ACADEMY OF SCIENCES PRESS. "Adriana Ocampo, The Space Geologist." I Was Wondering: A Curious Look at Women's Adventures in Science, October 2015. https://web.archive.org /web/20151015050422/http://www.iwaswondering.org/adriana_homepage.html.

OCAMPO, Adriana. *Geology and Emplacement Mechanism of Chicxulub Crater Deposits: An Analogue for Planetary Impact Ejecta*. VU University, Amsterdam, The Netherlands, March 25, 2013. https://web.archive.org/web/20150613035932/http://dare.ubvu.vu.nl/handle/1871/40118.

PHILLIPS, Tony. "In Search of Crater Chains." *NASA Science News*, May 12, 2006. https://science.nasa. gov/science-news/science-at-nasa/2006/12may_craterchains/.

SIMON, Yara. "Adriana Ocampo Is One of the Sheroes Behind NASA's Mission to Jupiter." *Remezcla*, July 15, 2016. http://remezcla.com/culture/adriana-ocampo-juno-jupiter-nasa/.

WILFORD, John Noble. "Dinosaur Theory: Sulfur Was Villain (but Hero for Humans)." *New York Times*, January 3, 1995. http://www.nytimes.com/1995/01/03/science/dinosaur-theory-sulfur-was-villain-but-hero-for-humans.html.

SUSAN SOLOMON

NATIONAL ACADEMY OF SCIENCE INTERVIEWS, Susan Solomon, atmospheric science, (recorded in 2002), http://www.nasonline.org/news-and-multimedia/podcasts/interviews/susan-solomon.html.

LAMONT DOHERTY EARTH OBSERVATORY. "Two Climate Scientists Win 2012 Vetlesen Prize for Work on Ozone Hole, Ice Cores." Columbia University & Earth Institute, January 14, 2013. http://www.ldeo .columbia.edu/news-eventstwo-climate-scientists-win-vetlesen-prize-work-ozone-hole-ice-cores.

REVKIN, Andrew C. "Scientist At Work: Susan Solomon—Melding Science and Diplomacy to Run a Global Climate Review." *New York Times*, February 6, 2007. http://query.nytimes.com/gst/fullpage .html?res=9C06E3DA133FF935A35751C0A9619C8B63&mcubz=3.

SOURCES

SCIENCE HISTORY INSTITUTE. "Susan Solomon." January 8, 2018.
    https://www.sciencehistory.org/historical-profile/susan-solomon.
VOLVO ENVIRONMENT PRIZE. "Susan Solomon." Volvo Environment Prize Foundation.
    http://www.environment-prize.com/laureates/by-year/2009/susan-solomon/.

CAROL GREIDER
BROOKS, Kelly. "With Bloomberg Distinguished Professorships, Johns Hopkins Aims to Foster Cross-
    specialty Collaboration." Johns Hopkins University, February 17, 2014.
    https://hub.jhu.edu/2014/02/17/bloomberg-distinguished-professors/.
CROCKETT, Kathy. "Success Stories: Carol Greider, Ph.D., Director of Molecular Biology & Genetics at
    Johns Hopkins University." The Yale Center for Dyslexia and Creativity, 2017.
    http://dyslexia.yale.edu/greider.html.
DREIFUS, Claudia. "On Winning a Nobel Prize in Science." *New York Times*, October 13, 2009.
    http://www.nytimes.com/2009/10/13/science/13conv.html.
GREIDER LAB. "Welcome to the Greider Lab." Johns Hopkins Medicine.
    http://www.greiderlab.org/index.html.
NOBEL PRIZE. "Carol W. Greider Biographical." NobelPrize.org, 2009.
    https://www.nobelprize.org/nobel_prizes/medicine/laureates/2009/greider-bio.html.
NUZZO, Regina. "Biography of Carol W. Greider." *Proceedings of the National Academy of Sciences of
    the United States of America*, June 7, 2005. https://doi.org/10.1073/pnas.0503019102.

MAY-BRITT MOSER
ABBOTT, Alison. "Neuroscience: Brains of Norway." *Nature*, October 6, 2014.
    http://www.nature.com/news/neuroscience-brains-of-norway-1.16079.
BRYCE, Emma. "The Brain Cartographer: May-Britt Moser Is Unlocking the Secrets of Our In-built GPS.
    Wired, May 28, 2017. http://www.wired.co.uk/article/mapping-human-brain-may-britt-moser.
COLUMBIA UNIVERSITY IRVING MEDICAL CENTER. "Horwitz Prize Awardees, 2013: May-Britt Moser, PhD."
    http://www.cumc.columbia.edu/research/horwitz-prize/prize-awardees.
GORMAN, James. "Profiles in Science: A Sense of Where You Are." *New York Times*, April 29, 2013. http://
    www.nytimes.com/2013/04/30/science/may-britt-and-edvard-moser-explore-the-brains-gps.html?_r=0.
NOBEL PRIZE. "May-Britt Moser Biographical." Nobelprize.org, November 13, 2017.
    http://www. nobelprize.org/nobel_prizes/medicine/laureates/2014/may-britt-moser-bio.html.
NTNU ADMINISTRATION. "'Best Female Boss'—Madame Beyer Award Goes to May-Britt Moser." NTNU
    Faculty of Medicine and Health Sciences. September 18, 2013. https://blog.medisin.ntnu.no
    /best-female-boss-madame-beyer-award-goes-to-may-britt-moser/?lang=en.
UNC SCHOOL OF MEDICINE. "Norwegian Scientists Win Perl-UNC Neuroscience Prize."
    UNC Neuroscience Center, January 3, 2013. https://www.med.unc.edu/neuroscience
    /norwegian-scientists-win-perl-unc-neuroscience-prize/.

SOURCES

MARYAM MIRZAKHANI

AMERICAN MATHEMATICAL SOCIETY. "A Tribute to Maryam Mirzakhani." 2017.
    http://www.ams.org/profession/mirzakhani/.

CALAMUR, Krishnadev. "Math's Highest Honor Is Given to a Woman for the First Time." NPR, August 13, 2014.
    https://www.npr.org/sections/thetwo-way/2014/08/13/340086786/maths-highest-honor-is-given-to
    -woman-for-the-first-time.

CHANG, Kenneth. "Maryam Mirzakhani, Only Woman to Win a Fields Medal, Dies at 40." *New York Times*,
    July 16, 2017. https://www.nytimes.com/2017/07/16/us/maryam-mirzakhani-dead.html.

HALPERN, Paul. "A Candle Illuminating the Dark." *Forbes*, August 1, 2017. https://www.forbes.com/sites
    /startswithabang/2017/08/01/maryam-mirzakhani-a-candle-illuminating-the-dark/#796c9b6e36c1.

HISTORY.COM EDITORS. "Iran-Iraq War." August 24, 2018. https://www.history.com/topics
    /middle-east/iran-iraq-war.

KLARREICH, Erica. "Meet the First Woman to Win Math's Most Prestigious Prize." *Wired*, August 13, 2014.
    https://www.wired.com/2014/08/maryam-mirzakhani-fields-medal/.

LAMB, Evelyn. "Mathematics World Mourns Maryam Mirzakhani, Only Woman to Win Fields Medal." *Scientific American*, July 17, 2017. https://www.scientificamerican.com/articleeraV
    /mathematics-world-mourns-maryam-mirzakhani-only-woman-to-win-fields-medal/.

MYERS, Andrew, and Bjorn Carey. "Maryam Mirzakhani, Stanford Mathematician and Fields Medal Winner,
    Dies." Stanford University, July 15, 2017. https://news.stanford.edu/2017/07/15
    /maryam-mirzakhani-stanford-mathematician-and-fields-medal-winner-dies/.

WRIGHT, Alex. "Maryam Mirzakhani (1977–2017)." *Science*, August 25, 2017.
    http://science.sciencemag.org/content/357/6353/758.

RAFI, Kasra. "Maryam Mirzakhani (1977–2017): Pioneering Mathematician and Winner of the Fields Medal."
    Nature, September 7, 2017. http://www.nature.com/nature/journal/v549/n7670/full/549032a
    .html?foxtrotcallback=true.

ROBERTS, Siobhan. "Maryam Mirzakhani's Pioneering Mathematical Legacy." *The New Yorker*, July 17, 2017.
    https://www.newyorker.com/tech/elements/maryam-mirzakhanis-pioneering-mathematical-legacy.

WOMEN IN SCIENCE GENERALLY

MCGRAYNE, Sharon Bertsch. *Nobel Prize Women in Science: Their Lives, Struggles, and Momentous
    Discoveries*. Washington, D.C.: Joseph Henry Press, 2001.

SWABY, Rachel. *Headstrong: 52 Women Who Changed Science—and the World*. New York: Broadway
    Books, 2015.

INDEX

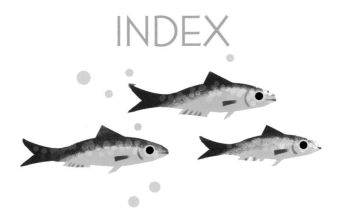

INDEX

INDEX

INDEX